# The House Hunt Game

# The House Hunt Game

## A GUIDE TO WINNING

### CAROLYN JANIK

MACMILLAN PUBLISHING CO., INC.

New York

Macmillan Publishing Co., Inc.
866 Third Avenue, New York, N.Y. 10022
Collier Macmillan Canada, Ltd.

Library of Congress Cataloging in Publication Data

Janik, Carolyn.
The house hunt game.

1. House buying. I. Title.
HD1379.J36      643      78-25608
ISBN 0-02-558970-9

First Printing 1979

Printed in the United States of America

*For Joe*
*whose love gave life to this book*

# Contents

ACKNOWLEDGMENTS      ix

INTRODUCTION—A WORD ABOUT THIS GAME      3

1.   GETTING READY TO BUY      9

2.   ALL-IMPORTANT LOCATION      27

3.   AGE, STYLE, AND LIVABILITY      56

4.   LOOKING FOR TROUBLE SPOTS      77

5.   WORKING WITH A SALES AGENT      94

6.   NEGOTIATING      109

7.   MORTGAGES      132

8.   THE CONTRACT AND THE CLOSING      155

THE LANGUAGE OF THE GAME      163

# Acknowledgments

Besides my husband, who believed even when believing was an act of pure faith, there are a few people who touched my life in a way that helped make this book a reality. I'd like to thank Leon and Genevieve Lech, my parents, who taught me to ask questions when I didn't know; Joe Vitali, who took the time to train an absolutely inexperienced salesperson and always had the time to answer his phone; Jack Hurley, who was tolerant of my working and not working while I was writing; and especially Richard Soloway, who said and taught that "success is the fulfillment of one's potential" and without whose encouragement I would not have begun.

# The House Hunt Game

# Introduction—
# A Word About This Game

With the exception of adventurous writers like George Plimpton, few of us would like to join the Detroit Lions on the playing field. Even with six-digit salaries at stake, the thought of getting run over by the likes of Joe Greene is unappealing at best. For the untrained, uninitiated, and unfit, the risks to life and limb are far too great. Better we should "participate" vocally in the stands or passively in front of our TV screens.

Yet there exists a twentieth-century game every bit as rough as football which most of us do jump into completely untrained and unprepared. With foolhardy abandon, we dash in and cheerfully join the other players running to and fro on a field where all the uniforms are similar and no one wears a number. Professionals, expert amateurs, and neophytes meet and mingle freely, and everyone is careful not to reveal his particular degree of experience. In fact, "playing dumb" is part of the strategy, a strategy which is surprisingly effective, for the rules of the game are many and subtle, but usually kept as secret as possible. The unspoken maxim of the experienced players seems to be, "Why tell the new guys how to play? They might score some points."

Equally deceptive is the almost universal rule which begins the game, "Be friendly!" One might say that the action always starts with a warm smile and a firm handshake. This congenial atmosphere usually lasts until the yardage markers begin to be counted off in dollars—or more accurately, in thousands of dollars. Then it's "Grab the ball and GO!—around, over, or

3

through anyone and anything you legally (and sometimes illegally) can."

Of course you already know that the name of the game is "House Hunt." Most people first play knowing little more than this name, yet they gamble every last cent they've been able to save upon it. Rarely does a beginner look at real estate as a game of financial investment where the stakes (both emotional and financial) are extremely high. Most young, and many not-so-young, couples are out to find their "dream home." They project onto the house all the emotionally laden overtones of the word "home" and are therefore often disappointed and sometimes devastated. Even second- and third-house buyers often forget that the goal of the game is to find an acceptable place to live. They respond emotionally to period decorating, color scheme, a white picket fence that reminds them of their childhood, a giant oak tree perfect for a tire swing, a beautiful view—the list is endless. They leave rational judgment behind and often success with it.

Ten years ago my husband and I first entered this game, a rather typical couple. Tired of apartment life and wanting a backyard where our toddler could play, we decided almost at the drop of a toy that we were ready to buy a house. The classified section of the daily and Sunday papers became prime reading material in our lives. Ads for houses that "sounded good" were circled in red, and it didn't take long before a real estate salesman in a nearby town had made a Sunday appointment with us.

This well-trained and expert sales agent "drove us around" the town and showed us churches, schools, shopping centers, and four overpriced and disappointing houses. We both felt bedraggled and discouraged. The man was showing us a fine, ideal community, but it was painfully obvious that *our* flimsy savings and beginner's salary could not buy a "home" in it.

Then, miraculously, our salesman remembered another house. As we entered the development where it was located, he was able to name and point out the homes of all the young doctors, lawyers, engineers, teachers, and future corporate executives who would be our neighbors. As we approached the front door, he knew and named every tree and shrub on the lot, explaining when it would flower to give the house "year-round color." He didn't need to say a word when we entered the immaculate, newly redecorated interior; but he knew the brand names of the carpet and drapery fabric. We were overwhelmed. The fact that it was necessary to walk through one tiny bedroom in order to get to another seemed absolutely insignificant; and since only one person (me) did the cooking, it didn't matter much that two people could hardly fit into the kitchen at the same time. We had found our dream home!

By the protective grace of a benevolent guardian angel, we had not taken our checkbook along.

"Perfectly all right," said our indomitable sales agent. "Just sign here and leave as a deposit whatever cash you have with you."

We should have felt an icy chill with those words, but we were too caught up in the hope and expectancy of *really* owning this beautiful HOME. After all, the salesman said that he thought he could get the sellers to come down $500 in price, and we were therefore pretty certain of getting it. We signed, leaving a deposit of $17!

Our ecstasy at having found our dream house faded more rapidly than Fourth of July Roman candles. That night both of us slept fitfully. We lay on opposite sides of our king-size bed, each afraid to toss and turn for fear of disturbing the other. We didn't know it, but the exact same fears were plaguing both our minds. Was this really the right house for us? Was this really a good time to buy? Was the price too high? Were the rooms too small? Did we want to live in that town? That neighborhood?

By some accident or miracle, one of us tentatively spoke up at breakfast. There followed a sense of absolute panic as we deluged each other with our every reservation and hesitation.

What had we done? Were the signatures on the offer form and the seventeen-dollar deposit binding? Would we have to go through with the deal, actually *buy* a house we didn't want? We did get our seventeen dollars back, and we didn't buy that "dream home." It wasn't until much later, however, when I was actually working in real estate myself, that I learned how close we had come to owning that house and the reason behind the return of our money. (No agreement is binding until a signed contract is in the hands of both parties or their attorneys. More about this later.)

Slightly singed but undaunted, we began "looking" again with several other brokers and finally bought a small ranch house with a lovely woods behind it. Our bid was still very close to the asking price and the "kindly" salesman did everything for us. We still knew little or nothing. After closing, we began homeownership with the sum total of $38.75 remaining in our bank account and an outstanding loan from our eighteen-month-old son for $124 (his entire savings account).

We were among the fortunate. The house was in good condition and, though we didn't know it then, priced fairly for the neighborhood. After living in it comfortably for five years and adding only a few amenities, we sold it in four days at an increase in price of almost fifty percent. We had gone in blind with every penny we had and we had come out not only unscathed but rather victorious.

We had played the House Hunt Game and won, not through skill, training, or experience, but by sheer luck. We had a good beginning; we would play again many times. Not all newcomers to the game are as fortunate, however. For some, their first game is devastating, leaving them unable to play or enjoy any of life's other games. They become slaves to their prize house, often because their payments are too high for their income or their maintenance problems are expensive and endless, sometimes because reselling would be too costly and/or difficult.

Like all games, there is no guaranteed formula for winning

in the House Hunt Game. Knowledge, experience, money, strategy, and self-control all help point the way to success, but I've seen some experienced people caught for huge losses because they chose the wrong play. And many, many times, I've seen young and inexperienced couples trampled by "old-timers" intent only on gain. Sometimes these new players felt the pain of feet running over them, but more often than not they stood up after the game dizzy and shaken, not really knowing what had happened.

So I come to the purpose of this book. It will not make you an expert, for experts in real estate are few and far between. But it may stand in for experience, which in this game can be very expensive and difficult to come by. If you are looking for a house as opposed to investment property, most of the other players you will meet on the field will be amateurs. The professionals will be the Realtors, sales agents, and lawyers. They too will bear watching, however, since they have a financial stake in *your* game. It is one of the confusing aspects of House Hunt that some of these professionals seem to play on both teams. So remember, if you want to play to win, wear your protective equipment at all times.

Perhaps I'm stressing the point too heavily. The vast majority of buyers, sellers, Realtors, sales agents, and lawyers are "nice guys"—sincere, honest, hard-working people. But money has a way of coloring the personality, and the House Hunt Game is big money. The best offense and the best defense are to be well informed, for no one can or will watch over your interests as well as you yourselves.

In the interest of being well informed, you may well ask at this point, "Who is this woman going on about a no-rules real estate game?" Actually I too am a sincere, honest, hard-working, somewhat experienced amateur/professional real estate player—one of the gang. In fifteen years as a "corporate wife," I have managed to survive the leasing of two apartments and the sale and purchase of five houses, one lakefront building lot, and one twelve-acre tract of land which we subdivided and resold. Along with moving and mothering, I have spent eight of those years working as a licensed real estate sales agent (a Realtor-Associate) in both Connecticut and New Jersey.

It didn't take me nearly that length of time to realize that in the real estate game nearly everyone knows (or thinks he knows) something and *no one* knows everything. I make no claims to expertise. I've been successful and I've been battered about somewhat in my own transactions, and I've been involved as an agent in many others—all kinds. The role of saleswoman has introduced me to some fine and wonderful people, and to some others.

What I offer you in this book is my experience. It is by no means complete and comprehensive, but it is a good beginning. Some of it is technical, some of it is funny, some of it is not so funny, and some of it is just plain horse sense that you may have overlooked.

# 1.

# Getting Ready to Buy

We all have our moments of fantasy. Who hasn't dreamed of returning the kick-off the full 100 yards? You are driving forward down the field; your pulse is pounding; the crowd is screaming wildly; the stadium erupts as you step across the goal line! You have scored!—a solitary hero, admired by all. Everyone wants a moment or two like this in life—a moment to say, "Look, Ma, I did it!"

There's something about buying your first house that corresponds in many ways to this fantasy. The house is like those goalposts at the end of a long field which you must run. Achieving it, you are at least a momentary victor. Home-ownership is a badge in our society, a mark of social status. The homeowner has attained that certain measure of success—property. The aura and status associated with this property ownership most likely grew from our feudal heritage. Those who worked the land were the poor, the peasants; those who owned the land were the wealthy, the landlords.

Even the medieval fairy tales you were told during your childhood assumed the innate "goodness" of property ownership. In true male chauvinist fashion, the goal or prize in most of these tales was the princess. The prince had to accomplish some impossible task or tasks and as a reward was given the princess. Then, and here's the relevant part, they rode off together to the prince's castle to live happily ever after. The existence of the castle was basic to the concept of happily ever after, and as such it was simply coupled with the idea of "happily" in a kind of coda to the tale. The action was *getting* the princess. That achieved, the happiness was guaranteed in the castle.

The twentieth-century version of this fairy-tale formula would be rather different. No longer are fair maidens *won* by earnest suitors. Couples meet and marry. The goal, the key to the dream of happily ever after, is not getting the princess, but getting the castle. The castle is now the climax of young love's tale, and with prices rising at their current rate, the tale should extend into middle age.

Although embroidered with magic and unreality, medieval fairy tales filled emotional needs in their hearers, for they dealt with elemental human situations. Is there something elemental then in Man's desire to possess a piece of the earth and a dwelling? So elemental that it is often linked in the mind with happiness? In terms of this book, is the home ownership goal at all valid?

Bear with me for just a bit, while I tell a twentieth-century fairy tale.

Young male and young female meet, fall in love, and marry. They ride off in their Pinto to their sparsely furnished one-bedroom apartment. Somewhere in the distance they catch sight of a modest but beautiful castle atop a sparkling glass mountain. They are told by the wizards of the world and both sets of parents that they too can own this castle; all they need do is climb the glass mountain and present the right number of golden apples to the gatekeeper.

Our couple begins saving every golden apple they can. When they have the right number, they climb the mountain. Exhausted, they reach the top. Here is their castle shining in the sun. But alas! it took so long to gather and save the golden apples that the *number* needed for the castle has gone up. They do not have enough and so stumble forlornly down the mountain.

It is harder to save golden apples now—baby detracts from

the gathering time. But both work at it, and finally, enough. Our couple climbs the mountain again. They again offer up their golden apples. "Sorry, still not quite enough." Rejection; dejection; defeat! They turn to leave. But wait. The gatekeeper is calling to them. Perhaps—just perhaps—he can work something out. There is a seemingly endless period of waiting while he talks with the owner-giant inside the castle. Footsteps.

"You are a fortunate family indeed," says the gatekeeper. "It just happens that the owner of this particular castle has already purchased a bigger and better castle in a distant land. Therefore he is willing—reluctant, but willing—to accept your offer."

Jubilation! Victory!

A long wait follows for "arrangements" and for the old owner to move out (three months). Now the couple and baby have their beautiful castle atop the sparkling glass mountain. Now it will surely be happily-ever-after.

But strangely and rather suddenly, the sparkling glass mountain is transformed into a battlefield. Armies of crab grass, dandelions, and clover fight each other for supremacy around the castle. The couple had never anticipated this terrible transformation. All their spare golden apples had been paid to the lawyer who took care of the "arrangements" for them. What to do about these warring weeds?

Aha! The magic golden apples, of course. So the couple buys and makes room in the castle stable for a chopper machine to keep the armies cut down to unrecognizable green stubs.

Then come the rains. Now the sparkling glass mountain becomes the great mudslide mountain, and the force of the running water penetrates the walls of the dungeon beneath the castle. The high-priced dungeon cleaning and waterproofing service must be called in (and paid for).

Meanwhile, inside the castle, things are not going much bet-

ter. So many broken places, so many dingy corners. Paint, new
wall tapestries, new floor coverings, new furniture, all are
*desperately* needed.

The story could go on and on. It is one I have seen replayed
a hundred times over. The couple is caught in the trap of
supporting their castle. They smile and nod and tell themselves and their friends and their families that they are happy.
And they are! Despite the problems and responsibilities,
choosing castle-buying almost always results in more "happiness" than choosing any of its alternatives.

What are the alternatives to castle-buying?

"Rent!" you say. "Easy mobility, no maintenance costs or
responsibilities, no taxes."

Not true. Or at least not entirely true. Mobility from one
apartment to another is considerably easier than from house to
house. There's no waiting period for the "right" buyer; there's
no delay for closing procedures; there's no real estate commission to pay. However, unless you have an exceptionally lenient and self-sacrificing landlord, most apartments now come
complete with a lease and a request for a sizable security deposit. (Some states set limits on these security deposits or require that interest be paid on excessive amounts. If you are
renting, it might be worthwhile to check the regulations in
your state.) Some leases specify that the security is forfeited if
the terms of the lease are violated in any way—this includes
early departure. Technically the landlord can also hold the
tenant responsible for the payment of rent for the entire duration of the lease since a lease is a contract. Few landlords are
willing to go to court over the point, however, since it is usually easier and cheaper to rent the apartment to another party,
but the possibility does exist.

"Of course," you say, "but there is always the possibility of
subletting in that case." This requires very careful screening
of your potential new tenant, since you, the original tenant, are
still responsible for the terms of the original lease. Because of
the obvious potential problems of subletting, most leases

specifically prohibit it. So we might agree that there is more mobility in renting, but not always *easy* mobility.

For the nonhandyman family, freedom from maintenance is a primary lure of the apartment. It is easy to forget, however, that the maintenance costs are very much included in the rent. Essentially you are paying for your maintenance services, yet you have *no* control over the promptness, efficiency, or quality of the work.

And taxes! *Every tenant pays real estate taxes.* True, it is the landlord who actually signs the tax payment check, but you can be certain that every tenant is contributing his fair share of those taxes in his rent. Every increase in taxes is passed along as an increase in rent. What's more, the landlord deducts the real estate taxes which he pays from his gross income on his federal income tax return, thus *lowering* the amount of income tax he must pay. Meanwhile the tenant simply pays out the additional money in rent with no tax relief whatsoever.

So much for the "advantages" of renting.

What about the disadvantages? Financial drain would probably take top honors. Renting simply devours a good portion of your monthly income with no redeeming financial advantages. Apartment rents are constantly increasing to keep pace with inflation. These increases drain your income and handsomely line the landlord's pockets, since his expenses (payments on the mortgage, etc.) do not increase in direct proportion.

Houses also respond to inflation, going ever upward in price with the decreasing value of the dollar. When you own a house, however, *your* monthly mortgage payment will remain fixed (except for tax increases) while the dollar value of your house rises to keep pace with inflation. (It can even race ahead of inflation with a little decorating and care.) Also, every mortgage payment you make adds to your equity in the house. This builds up slowly at first but gathers momentum with each passing year.

Privacy would be right in there competing with financial

drain for first place in the disadvantage category. In apartments, it is always minimal. You can hear every pot bang in your neighbor's kitchen, not to mention the raised voices and crying children. And if you're an outdoor type, it's rather disconcerting to have the neighborhood cowboys and Indians tearing through your barbecue. Even gin and tonic won't completely soothe over this disadvantage.

There exists yet another detriment to renting which is less tangible but perhaps equally important. Some element in the human psyche (perhaps related to animalistic territorial rights) needs to proclaim with pride, "This is mine!" Homeownership obviously satisfies this need; renting does not. In an apartment, the primal cry of "This is mine!" can only relate to the possessions within the apartment.

Responding unconsciously to this need for pride in possession, many couples spend a great deal on quality furnishings. Besides cutting into their ability to save money toward a down payment, the furniture actually hampers their house hunting. I have heard many first-home buyers say, "Oh, I *love* this house, but where can I put my antique dining room set? Or my king-size bed and triple dresser?" etc. Choice of style in houses is usually most limited in the lower price ranges where most people begin. So their expensive possessions further restrict the possibilities for many couples.

"Okay," you say, "renting isn't too great. How about a 'condo'?"

Condominiums: Low, low down payments! Swimming pools! Recreation complexes! Tennis courts! Homogeneous communities! Beautiful landscaping! No outdoor maintenance work! You've seen the ads. Sounds like the ideal castle.

So thought my brother and his wife. My brother is two years younger than I, and by the time he was married a year or two, we were already into our first home and caught up in fixing up the basement, mowing the lawn, digging the weeds, worrying about the septic tank (which did later have to be replaced), and hoping the carpeting would last a few more years.

I remember sitting one holiday in our parents' living room, talking with my brother and his wife.

"Yes," they beamed, "we found this great new condo! It has three bedrooms, two baths [and this, and that, and even another—]. All that with no maintenance and no worries."

"But it's just like renting," we ventured.

"Oh, no! This is the *modern* way to live," they said, somewhat condescendingly.

My husband and I became quiet and the subject was changed. We went to their housewarming a month or so later, and we duly admired the sliding glass doors to their walled private patio, the sparkling new kitchen peninsula that divided dining area from working area, the two bathrooms, the superample parking areas all around them, and the Olympic-sized pool being built next to the proposed site of the huge recreation complex.

Our pillow talk that night ended in betting that gave them a year to eighteen months. We both lost. They sold and moved into a house in nine months.

Why? Well—who makes the rules at a condo complex? When are the children allowed in the pool? Who decides, those with children or those without? Who owns the ground upon which the children play (or fight)? Who was it who said the walls were soundproof? Who governs the use of the "extra" parking areas? What games should be purchased for the recreation complex? Who supervises? You don't need any more. The glass mountain around this castle may have sparkled in the distance, but not up close.

Among our friends are an economist and his wife who avoided the lure of the condo completely. Near the beginning of their house-hunting time, they had come upon an article in a professional journal concerning condominiums. The results of an economic and sociological study had shown that the overwhelming majority of people in condos were markedly unhappy. Only in a few select situations (usually very high-priced condos) were the majority of the owners satisfied.

There were many complaints about builders not fulfilling their promises, inferior maintenance, haphazard services, lack of privacy, shoddy construction, and a distaste for the constant appeal to the will of the majority.

All this sounds very "down" on condos, and I must take a minute here to mention some saving graces. Condos do have most of the disadvantages of apartment living, but they also have some of the advantages of homeownership. You can mortgage a condo just as you would mortgage a home, and in the case of new condos, most builders have prearranged for financing, so you can often get the mortgage with a minimal down payment. This puts you into the Homeowner Game with very little cash outlay. You can begin to reap the advantages of appreciation in value and tax-deductible interest and real estate tax payments. (Interest and taxes paid out are deductible from gross income on your federal income tax return, just as they are for the apartment landlord or the private homeowner.) Although mobility is somewhat decreased, since you must sell the condo as you would a house, the profit from that sale will usually provide a good down payment on your next condo or on a house. For those who prefer to live in major cities, condos may be the only way to actually own a piece of real estate, and for those couples just starting out, condos can be a pathway into the game with a very small down payment. A condo may not make you any happier than living in an apartment, but your money will be growing.

Since you are reading this book, however, let's assume that you have your heart set on a separate house. Even if you are in the getting-ready stage and short of down payment money for the kind of house you have in mind, you can still enjoy the House Hunt Game—and profitably at that.

House Hunt is a game where everyone and anyone is allowed on the field at will. Not everyone is playing, but it is *extremely* difficult to tell the sightseers, the observers, the warm-ups, and the actual players apart. So even if you are short of down-payment cash and therefore unable to buy, you can gain immeasurably in knowledge and self-confidence by pseudoparticipation in the game. The advantage, of course, is that you *cannot* get hurt, financially or emotionally, since you aren't really playing.

First of all, unless you have time to kill or wish to look at the latest in decorating or kitchen appliances, avoid "model homes" on new tracts. You will get an idea of the price tag on new construction in your area, but that's all. Also avoid home-owner ads at this stage or you will waste a great deal of time hunting down locations and fending off anxious sellers.

Instead, open the classified section of your local newspaper and pick a broker-advertised house that sounds appealing in your general price range. Dial the broker's number and tell the salesman that you are interested in seeing the house advertised. You're guaranteed to get a warm reception and an agent anxious to make an appointment, at your convenience, to see that house and several others similar to it.

By going out onto the House Hunt field and "exercising" in this way about once a month, you will build know-how and stamina for the real game to come. You will become familiar with the various towns in your area, and you will begin to get a "feel" for the dollar value in each town and even in specific neighborhoods. You will also have the opportunity to work with some real estate salespeople and evaluate their competence. (You may want to go looking with some of these people again, and some you may never want to see again.)

Your most important tactic during these warm-up sessions is asking questions—and asking the same questions of different salespeople. You will find the differences in their answers very enlightening.

Some starter questions might be: What's the most popular style house in this area? (You want to know this because you will probably want to sell at some point in the future.) Which town in the area has the most services for the tax dollar? Which town is growing fastest? (You're wondering if more schools will soon be needed. More schools mean more taxes.) Which towns have the most industry? (Industry is generally good tax support.) What kind of industry? Where is it located? Which neighborhoods sell best? *Why*? Where are the schools? Are the children bused? Do they return home for lunch? Where are the playgrounds, parks, and shopping centers? Can you give me a street map of the town? County? (This is very valuable for snooping on your own, and for locating houses you have seen.) How much down payment are the banks in the area requiring? At what interest rate? (A good sales agent will be able to give you the name of the bank and its current requirements.) And the most important questions of all: Have there been any homes sold in this neighborhood recently? *How much did they sell for*? This information is invaluable and a well-trained salesperson who is in touch with the market will gladly give it to you.

When you return home after your warm-up trips, take a few minutes to keep a House Hunt notebook. Write down the broker's or real estate company's name and the name of the salesperson. (You might even attach his card.) Make a short evaluation of him or her as a potential agent for future house hunts. Then keep a list of all the houses you looked at, with location, price, style, and your evaluation. Also keep a list of the selling prices of the other houses in the neighborhood. When you are ready to play House Hunt in earnest, this notebook will be worth many years of experience. You will be able to look up those "old" houses you saw in your warm-up days and ask important questions of the salesperson with whom you are currently working: Are the houses still for sale? Why? If sold, *what did they sell for*? How long did it take to sell them? This information can and will save you from paying too much for a house, so take the time to keep the notebook!

Many couples who are still getting ready to buy are apprehensive about going out with a sales agent. They imagine themselves stuck with the original supersalesman on their backs—calling every day, pushing one house or another. This is simply not an accurate picture. An agent is in real estate *to make money.* He does not particularly enjoy driving people around in his car (especially at today's gas prices) and walking in and out of houses he has already seen five or six times. Therefore no salesman ("good" or "bad") will spend his time on people who cannot possibly buy. So in this case, honesty *is* the best policy. After you have seen several houses, ask about down payment requirements, even if you know this information cold. Then, near the end of your day, simply tell the salesman that you appreciate his time, but that you realize now that you do not yet have a large enough down payment to buy. If you liked working with him, tell him so and say that you will contact him in X months, when you should be ready. Or ask him to contact you from time to time. I guarantee that if you tell a salesman that you *cannot* buy at the present time, you will not be bothered again.

Now these tactics may not win you any popularity contests among real estate people, but popularity is not the object of the game. Your main objectives at this point are to gain perspective on the market as a whole and to learn to evaluate individual houses. It is hard, tiring work which loses its glamour quickly, so don't do too much of it all at once. But do it!

During these warm-up sessions, you will no doubt see houses that you "fall in love with." You may even think that you have found your dream house, and you will be unable to buy it. You will then have to work through your feelings of impatience, frustration, resentment, and just plain sadness. But this too is beneficial, for you will begin to conquer that sense of urgency which salesmen everywhere use to help sell, sell, *sell*! As long as you feel that "this is the one and only and I must have it no matter what," you are vulnerable, and that sense of urgency will definitely cost you money.

Let's assume that you do see your dream house and come away longing for it. My experience has proved over and over again that *two* other dream houses, perfect for you, will come on the market within the next few months. The House Hunt

Game is very much like the Love and Marriage Game; many a broken heart has stopped aching when another lover appeared on the scene. Just as each person has many potential marriage partners in the world, each couple has many potential "right" houses. And just as some marriages work well for a while and then fall apart, so some houses are right at one stage of life and all wrong at another. Fortunately it is *usually* easier to sell a house than to get a divorce.

During the period of time in which you are getting ready to buy, it is important that you begin to know your own strengths and weaknesses. How much cash do you really need to get into this game? And how much can you afford to pay out each month and still qualify for the "lived happily ever after" coda? Knowing these answers *before* you start to play seriously can save much pain and strain in a marriage and facilitate real happiness in that dream house.

Every serious variant of the House Hunt Game except one requires a sizable cash outlay, the down payment, in order to begin playing. Banks and mortgage companies are businesses, and giving mortgages is for them an investment upon which they will get a certain rate of return (interest). Their aim is to make these investments with minimal risk. In the event that a couple defaults on its mortgage, the bank must foreclose. The foreclosure procedure is rather expensive, and because the bank wants to be certain that it will get its money out of the house after foreclosure costs, real estate commissions, unpaid taxes, etc., they will not lend the total purchase price. Therefore a down payment is required as investment protection.

The one exception to the down payment requirement is the VA mortgage. (VA stands for Veterans Administration.) If *either* of you is a veteran and qualifies for a VA mortgage (you must check with your VA office for qualification requirements), you can actually buy a house with *no money down*.

Before you rush off to join the army, let me clarify a little further. The Veterans Administration will *guarantee* a mortgage for the full appraised value (which is usually, but not always, near or at the purchase price) of a home for a qualified veteran. (They will do this only once for each vet.) There are limitations on this guarantee, but they will be covered in the chapter on mortgages. Note carefully, however, that the VA does *not* give the mortgage. It guarantees the mortgage to a conventional lending institution—usually a bank, a savings and loan association, or a mortgage company. This makes the whole procedure somewhat less than gloriously simple. The maximum interest rate for VA mortgages is set by federal law and therefore is not always appealing to competitive local institutions. There is also considerable red tape involved with a VA mortgage which often delays the closing, and the VA can be rather strict about your income and credit standing. But if you can get by all this, you really can buy a house without any cash down.

Some couples with small down payments go the route of the condo; others use the help of another federal program sponsored by the FHA (Federal Housing Administration). The FHA does not give mortgages either—it insures them. The insurance costs you, the buyer, one-half of one percent in additional interest rate each month. But because of this insurance, banks and lending institutions are willing to make loans with smaller down payments. Practically anyone can get an FHA mortgage, if they meet FHA qualification requirements (job security, income, credit standing, etc.). You can obtain information on the current requirements from your local FHA office. The FHA, however, has set maximum dollar amounts which they will insure, and this effectively sets the upper limits on house prices for many couples. You may purchase a house which costs more than these upper limits, but you must make up the difference in cash. All FHA mortgages require some down payment, and it is on a sliding scale—but let me save these details also for the mortgage chapter. Enough to know now that the possibility of low down payment buying does exist.

VA and FHA mortgages can get complicated; but remember that even the most complex tasks can be made simple if a good coach walks you through step by step, pointing out and smoothing over the rough spots. If you think you may be playing House Hunt with VA or FHA help, be extra careful in choosing your salesman *and* the broker he works for. Experience and reputation *really* count in these variations of the game.

On the other hand, if you're not a vet and you don't want to pay the usually higher interest rates of FHA mortgages, you are probably wondering just how much cash you will need to get into this game. The answer, an elusive one, depends on the size and shape of your goal (the house) and on your condition (financial). Each and every lending institution sets its own guidelines. Usually they require a minimum of twenty percent of the purchase price of a house as the down payment, although I've heard of banks giving mortgages with fifteen or even ten percent down in "good times" (easy money times). Specialized mortgage companies sometimes have special insured loans with lower down payments also, but the insurance usually costs money. This all varies tremendously from locality to locality and from time to time and is another instance where a good salesman who knows all aspects of his job can be worth literally ten times his weight in dollars.

When times are "bad" (tight money), I've seen the down payment requirements go up to thirty, thirty-three-and-a-third, and even fifty percent of the purchase price, thus effectively excluding most buyers and closing the money market. This is usually the time to put actual buying out of mind, save as much as possible, and get lots of warm-up experience. It is also the time, however, when there are many *real* bargains available. Sellers who *must* sell are caught by the shortage of mortgage money and therefore the shortage of potential buyers. If during a period of tight money you should find a real estate broker who has an inside track on some available financing, you may get a *super* bargain.

The other main criterion for getting into the game, your

financial condition, is every bit as important as the size of your down payment. With a large down payment, some banks will "overlook" a bit of shakiness in financial condition. Their investment is protected by your cash outlay. With a very stable and healthy financial picture, on the other hand, some banks may squeeze a bit on the percentage of down payment required. Banks are run by people in order to make money, and rules, therefore, are made to be broken—or at least relaxed a little.

You may be reeling by now and wondering if getting into this game is worth the trouble. And rightly so, for the financing of houses is by far the most technical and complicated part of the game. But a little knowledge before you begin can save you much aimless wandering about looking at houses far out of your price range. It can also save you the shock of a mortgage rejection after a careless or incompetent agent talks you into a house which you cannot possibly afford.

Briefly and generally, qualification (the ability to get a mortgage and buy a house) depends upon the relationship of your income to the principal, interest, and tax payment you will have to make each month. A general rule of thumb is that the total of mortgage payment (principal and interest), taxes, and fire insurance per month should not be greater than your *combined gross* annual income divided by 60. So a couple with a combined gross annual income of $24,000 could spend up to $400 per month on housing ($24,000 ÷ 60 = $400).

Some lending institutions allow the gross annual income divided by 50 ($25,000 ÷ 50 = $500 per month). Again this varies from locality to locality *and* from one bank to another. You can find out the prevalent guidelines in your area by simply calling a savings bank or two. The conversation might go something like this:

"Good afternoon. Rainy Day Savings Bank."

"Good afternoon. May I speak to someone in the mortgage department?"

"New or existing?"

"Pardon?"

"Does your question pertain to a new or existing mortgage, sir?"

"Oh, a new mortgage."

"One moment."

New voice: "Mrs. Details speaking."

"Yes, my name is Mr. Tenant. We are considering purchasing a house. Would you be able to tell me the bank's qualification guidelines for getting a mortgage?"

Mrs. Details will be only too happy to answer all your questions. Banks *want* to make loans—this is their business. It is how they make a profit.

This discussion of financing is but the tip of the iceberg. I will try to be considerably more explicit and comprehensive when we discuss actually getting the mortgage. For the time being, however, let this information help you decide when to start playing House Hunt in earnest and which league to play in.

If you decide that you are not yet ready to buy, you may begin to find the getting-ready period very frustrating. Your friends may be out there on the field actually playing; some might even score goals and buy; and there you sit, hunched over, watching. Try to be patient during this time. Enjoy your warm-up times out on the field and learn from them and from your friends. When you do begin to play, you will be competing against sellers and other buyers with a wide range of experience. If you spend the getting-ready time carefully, it may make the difference between simply buying a house and actually winning at the game—that is, being happy with that house and selling it later at a handsome profit.

If you are a potential first-house buyer, you do have one definite advantage over many experienced players who are forced to buy because their former houses have been sold or because they have been transferred by their companies. This advantage is time—*not* an insignificant element of this game. If you are in an apartment, you may be able to extend your lease in short intervals, perhaps three or four months at a time, giving you the freedom to find the right house without time pressure and the ability to negotiate with occupancy as a factor (to your benefit, of course). More about this when we get to negotiation.

The time of year can also work to the advantage of the first-home buyer. House Hunt is a seasonal game in most areas of the United States, but sometimes off-season play can be the most profitable of all. If you would like to begin home-ownership with a superbargain, you might try aiming toward one of real estate's "dead" seasons. You do this by beginning to look seriously in the fall, September and October. Keep tabs on all the acceptable houses you see, but do not buy, since September and October are very good sales months, second only to March, April, and May. Return to see those houses still available at the end of November or beginning of December. This is panic time for most sellers, expecially if the house is vacant. Visions of heating bills, furnace and water problems, broken pipes, storm damage, etc., stampede through their heads. Any buyer, and often any remotely reasonable offer, looks beautiful at this time of year.

If you choose this off-season play, you must be very strong while you are out on the field in the fall. You will see houses which you may "just love" and want very much to buy, *and* you may lose them. Someone else may pay the price and take the prize. But there are others; there will always be others. House Hunt is a gambling game, and patience is usually very well rewarded.

Off-season is also the time when there are the smallest number of listings (houses for sale) on the books. So if your dream house gets sold for top dollar in October and you find nothing in November that interests you, settle down and enjoy the holidays in your apartment. As spring approaches, there will be a whole raft of new listings tumbling onto the market, and you will be so much the wiser for having been shopping through the fall.

Although it is not quite so dramatic, because the weather is milder, the summer is another dead time in real estate. Many people are away on vacation and as a result buyers are not so plentiful. Sellers who do not have their houses sold by June begin worrying if they will be "out" in time for their children to change schools, etc. A house that you see and like in April may sell for several thousand dollars less in July. Money and price should not be your sole considerations when you play House Hunt, but it does no harm to keep these factors in mind.

As your getting-ready time approaches an end, I want to stress again that the greatest mistake made by most first-house buyers is the belief that there is a "perfect house" out there waiting for them. This is analogous to thinking that one must search the world over for one's perfect mate. Happiness can be found with many mates and many houses, and perfect ones in either category are about equally rare.

# 2.

# All-Important Location

Driving buyers from one house to another is an excellent test for the extrovert personality. There you have three persons (usually a married couple and the sales agent) essentially locked in the car together. The couple is stiff, somewhat suspicious, and defensive; the agent is trying to be "friendly" while very much aware that, as a complete stranger, he is about to share in a very personal experience—the search for a home. All this usually without benefit of introduction, mutual friends, or even references. It's no wonder that people put on their masks and fortify their social walls.

As the formality and defensiveness wear off, however, buyers begin to sit more comfortably in their seats. Sensing this, the sales agent can begin to assume the role of coach for the House Hunt Game. With the growth of trust, the couple's questions become more open and invariably focus on their concern for "getting a good deal."

"What's the most important thing to look for in a house?" In one form or another this is *the* question. In it is the essence of the player/coach House Hunt Game relationship, for it really asks a much larger question. It really says, "Tell us what you know about surviving in this game."

No one honestly wants to hear a three-hour lecture on the principles of real estate, so when the question is asked of me, my reply is always the same: "There are three really important things in real estate: location, location, and location."

This little quip is not an original insight of mine but one of

those well-known axioms that float around in every sport, profession, or occupation. It avoids the three-hour lecture, yet it
also strikes the core of what really matters. You can fix up,
enlarge, or tear down and rebuild a house, but you can't do
much about moving or restructuring the ground that it stands
upon, and you have even less ability to influence the area
surrounding your lot. It is that small piece of earth that can
make or break you in the game of House Hunt.

Translated, that "location, location, and location" equates
to town, neighborhood, and lot. It is easy for me to tell you,
"These are the three most important elements in your choice,"
but it is much more difficult to answer the question, "What's
right?" In other words, you ask, "How do I win by putting my
money on location? What is the *right* town, neighborhood, or
lot?" Here I must give you an answer which, in its very truth,
sounds evasive: The question of "What is right? Is this a winning house?" represents the subtlety, the complexity, and
even part of the excitement of the House Hunt Game. There
are no *guaranteed* right answers. Winning is really a matter of
personal belief; winning is the achievement of *your* personal
goal.

To understand this definition of winning in House Hunt,
you must ask yourself, "Am I looking for a house that will suit
me individually no matter what, or do I want a house that I
can resell for a profit?" If you plan to remain in a house
more or less permanently, you can please yourself with little
or no concern about resale. You must take care only to be
sure that what you see is really what you want. This requires knowledge of what homeownership in general en-
tails and what the ownership of this particular house will
mean. Through the information you can gather, you must be
able to project what life in a particular house will be like.
Then you must have enough self-knowledge to answer the
question, "Will this please us?"

If, however, you are playing the transient version of House
Hunt, if you plan or know that you will move in the next two to

five years, the measure of your victory in this game will be not only your happiness in the house, but also the speed and profit with which you can sell it. In this case, you must judge both what it will be like to live in the house and how *other* buyers will respond to it when you are ready to sell.

As coach for your game, I will try throughout the next several chapters to point out those factors which might affect your satisfaction with a house. To the evaluations and information that can be determined by observation or research, I'll try to add what I have learned about "buyer opinion" while observing people in the act of seeking and buying houses. So set out and keep in mind your personal goals in this game, and let's dig into the all-important question of location.

Towns (actually municipalities, for we are talking about everything from major cities to rural areas) are as different as people. Just like the citizens that make them up, they have stature, personality, problems, and character. Choosing one is in many ways like choosing a friend; there must be some basis for compatibility in your makeups.

When comparing one town to another, House Hunt players invariably ask two questions: "What are the taxes?" and "How are the schools?" The reply to the tax question is the hard, cold reality of numbers, and on this basis it is easy to make valid and intelligent comparisons. Schools are another story. It is a rare occasion when you will receive any answer other than "Oh, yes! We have very good schools!" What other response can a sales agent make? *Everyone* wants good schools.

Before we go into the fine points of school evaluation, let's sit down around the blackboard and go over taxes. As I said, these are a matter of numbers, and it's difficult to make an error in this department if your figures are accurate. All tax information is a matter of public record and is therefore easy to come by. Here I suggest extensive use of the phone. You can obtain much information by simply calling the tax collector's or assessor's office.

When it comes down to the nitty-gritty, taxes can be the

factor which determines whether or not you can afford your dream house. As you read in the previous chapter, banks base their mortgage approvals upon the total monthly payment required to carry a house in relation to your income. If your dream house is located in a town with a high tax rate, those payments can be fifty or even seventy-five dollars a month higher than the same house located in a town with a low tax rate. That fifty dollars could make the difference between getting the mortgage you want and getting a polite refusal.

Numbers are not the be-all and end-all, however. In comparing tax rates, you must ask yourself what you get for your money. Take into consideration sewers, garbage collection, police and fire protection, recreation, and of course schools. To start your town comparisons, make a list of all the towns under consideration and then apply the same questions to each one. Write down the information you obtain either in chart form or on separate sheets for each town.

Let's start at the beginning: the mill rate. This is the basic tax rate. A mill is one-tenth of one cent. In terms of money, it is the actual dollar figure which you pay on each $1,000 of tax assessment. For simplicity, let's assume you own a house assessed at the improbable figure of $10,000. If the town's mill rate is 1.5, it means that you must pay $1.50 a year for each $1,000 of tax assessment, or in this example $15 ($1.5 \times 10 = 15$). This is of course the impossible dream! Most mill rates and most assessments are considerably higher. In reality your mill rate might be something like 24.9 and your assessment $43,750. In this case your taxes would be $24.9 \times 43.75 = 1,089.375$ or an annual tax of $1,089.38. Here you are paying $24.90 for each $1,000 of assessment, or 43 thousands plus 75 percent of a thousand. It really isn't difficult if you just keep track of the decimal points.

Understanding assessed value is just as important as understanding mill rate. To determine assessed value, the town sends out assessors, usually a professional company, to evaluate each property inside and out. Then by comparison they determine the "fair market value" of that property. Fair market value is the price at which the assessor thinks the house would sell on the open market.

Some towns base their tax rates on full value assessment. This means that the mill rate is simply multiplied times the number of thousands, as I just explained. Other towns, however, base their mill rates on a percentage of the assessed value. In a town with a mill rate based upon 60 percent of assessed value, you must first take 60 percent of the full assessment and then multiply that figure times the mill rate. In the case of the house I used in the previous example, the assessed value was $43,750. Sixty percent of this is $0.60 \times 43,750 = 26,250$. Then the mill rate of 24.9 is multiplied by the 60 percent figure (26,250). Thus in this town where taxes are based upon 60 percent of assessed value, the actual tax payment would be $653.63 a year ($24.9 \times 26.25 = 653.625$).

Most real estate listings have all this information worked out for you and the agent simply glances down at his tables and gives you the exact dollar figure. This is all well and good, but it is to your advantage to understand the tax structures of the towns you are considering. No two houses are exactly alike, so it is difficult to compare the taxes on a house-to-house basis. It is not difficult, however, to compare tax *structure* from one town to another.

The task of assessing the value of every piece of property in a town is obviously time-consuming and expensive. Most towns therefore assess periodically, usually every ten years, but in some places less frequently. Since taxes are contingent upon assessment, it is important to ascertain when the last assessment was done in the towns you are considering and when reassessment is planned. Keep in mind that reassessment can often mean significant change in the amount of tax upon a piece of property. For example, we bought the house where we now live while the reassessment was in process. Six months after we moved in, we received notice from the bank that our monthly mortgage payment was to be increased by thirty-two dollars as a result of the tax revaluation. This sudden jump is not always the case, however. In an older home, taxes might even go down as a result of revaluation, particularly if the house is in poor condition when the revaluation is done. (You can fix it up later.)

Mill rate and assessment determine the number of dollars that you must pay to the town each year. In return for these dollars, the town provides services for you. The real question is how these services compare from town to town. In other words, how much do you get for your dollar? In one Connecticut town where we lived, we had to pay a private service to collect our garbage and another service to have our septic tank cleaned. The town line was three houses down the street, and the people living beyond it in the neighboring town had both garbage collection and septic tank cleaning provided by the municipality. And *theirs* was the lower tax rate!

School costs consume the largest part of the tax dollar in almost all communities. But before we delve into all the complexities of evaluating the schools, let's look at the other services which are generally dependent upon taxes.

In terms of potential cost to the homeowner, waste disposal looms among the largest of these. If a town which you are considering is suburban or rural, part or all of it may dispose of waste through the use of septic tanks. In areas with good drainage and light population density, these systems are certainly adequate. However, as population density increases, towns may find it necessary to install sewers, and sewers cost money.

Sewers can be financed in several ways. A town may decide to install sewers throughout its entire area and add the cost of installation and maintenance to the general taxes, thus increasing the tax rate for everyone. Or the individual homeowner may be assessed for his portion of the cost of sewers in his particular area. This assessment is generally made per running foot across the front line of the property and can be very expensive. Many buyers are reluctant to consider property where sewers are imminent because they do not want to face these high assessments immediately after the financial strain of purchasing the house itself. This reluctance is so common that many sellers state in writing when listing their property for sale that they agree to pay the sewer assessment in full at closing. If this offer is not made in writing on the sales listing, it is a point that can be negotiated and the price of the house adjusted accordingly.

Yet another method of financing sewers is that the town absorbs the cost of installation but then charges an annual "sewer use fee" in addition to normal taxes. This type of sewer tax usually appears on a real estate listing under the heading of special fees or taxes. The annual cost is usually not great (generally about $75 or $100) and this type of fee does not usually discourage buyers since they will be paying for sewers only as long as they own the house. The next owner will simply take up the cost of sewer use when he buys the house.

No matter how the sewers are financed, the homeowner usually pays for the hookup to the sewer line in the street. If sewers are imminent in an area which you are considering, you will have to plan on the out-of-pocket cost of hookup (which usually runs into several hundred dollars) and on some kind of increased taxes to finance them.

Most, but not all, towns provide garbage pickup as a municipal service. Where it is not provided, however, be sure to inquire about the cost of private collection, since you must include that figure in your monthly expenditures. In towns where the service is included in your taxes, inquire how often the collections are made—you will appreciate the twice-a-week collection if you have ever lived with a week's accumulated garbage!

Stop for a moment also to look at the police and fire protection in the towns you are considering. Is the fire department a full-time one or volunteer? If volunteer, is there at least a minimum duty force twenty-four hours a day? If so, a volunteer department is not a detriment; many do an outstanding job. There is often a neighborhood feeling and a great *esprit de corps* among the men. Our own department surprised us our first Christmas in New Jersey when we saw Santa driven from house to house on a big red engine, giving out candy canes to all the neighborhood children.

You might inquire how large the police force is and how this number compares with the population and its density. How many cars and what special rescue vehicles do they use? Are the police officers rescue-trained? Is there an ambulance squad in the town?

As you drive around the town, look at the streets. Are they well maintained and clean? Clean streets in spring, summer, and fall bespeak a good road maintenance department and are a clue to the promptness and efficiency of snow removal in winter.

Think also about recreation as you tour each town. Is there a community swimming pool? Does it require an additional membership fee or is it free to town residents? Are there indoor swimming facilities available to all school children? What planned programs are conducted in the schools? Are school facilities open to the public when classes are not in session? Does the town sponsor free sports instruction programs for both children and adults? Is the library a hush-hush reference place or an active community center?

Apart from the community services paid for by taxes, you might also ask: Is there a hospital in or near the town? Adequate medical and dental services within reasonable distance? A YMCA? Movie theatres? Museums? Art, music, or dance groups? Good shopping? In other words, are the activities that are meaningful to you obtainable and convenient?

If you think that I'm beginning to sound more like a League of Women Voters community researcher than a real estate agent, please bear with me a bit. I'm aware that no *one* of these factors would (or should) deter you from buying a house which was satisfactory to you in a majority of important considerations, but taken together they create a mural of life in the town you are choosing. And once you actually buy a house, you become part of the pattern of life in that town, like it or not.

While I'm standing here at the blackboard playing "Town Hunt Coach," let me throw out just a few more questions for your consideration. My concern at this point is the growth potential of the towns which you are considering. The factor of growth potential cannot be pinned down to concrete numbers as are taxes, but it is ever so important to you, especially if you plan to remain in your house for a number of years.

As you evaluate the present character of a town, you want to ask, "Where is this town headed? What kind of town will it be in five, ten, or twenty years?" Like all predictions of the future, the answer to these questions begins with a search of the past. Does the town show evidence of past planning or is it a hodgepodge of juxtaposed incongruous areas? Has industry been encouraged? What industry is now in the town? Where is it located? Was there planning for growth and added industry?

Perhaps a town is fully developed with no open land for further development. In this case, has the tax rate been stable for a number of years? What are the possibilities of redevelopment and renewal areas? High-rise apartments? High-density housing? Could the schools handle the extra population that high-density housing would bring? Is there a creeping, growing slum area, or are the older sections of the town maintained with dignity and pride?

On the other hand, a town may be rural with a great deal of farmland and undeveloped open space. In this case you cannot help but wonder how much of this land will be sold off to housing developers and how soon. Will schools and town services be able to handle the addition of these developments? Or will new taxes be necessary? No new homeowner wants to live in a town where he will face substantial tax increases year after year. Therefore, as you drive about, try to look into the crystal ball a bit and visualize "your" town in ten years.

Speaking of crystal balls, as I write this I can see in mine some readers sitting with note pads out calculating tax dollars as compared to services in various towns. Others, however, have already turned the pages ahead to see how much longer I'm going to go on about tax dollar value. Well, relax, I'm about to leave the numbers for a while. Those of you who were fingering pads and pencils might jot down the phone numbers for the tax collector's and assessor's offices, where you will easily obtain all the figures you need—including exactly what anyone in the town pays in property tax.

I would like at this point to put aside my House Hunt Coach's hat for a few moments and talk more conversationally about schools. But first I have a small confession to make. Despite the fact that I am writing this book, I never chose real estate as a career. It "happened" to me. We had overextended our finances by buying, with a sizable short-term mortgage, a lakefront lot. A payment of $1,000 was due on that mortgage in four months, and we simply did not have the money. I *needed* a high-paying part-time job with flexible hours that would allow me to be with my children. (Not easy to come by!) It happened, however, that a large real estate firm was opening a branch office in our town. They were so desperately in need of salespeople to staff it that they were willing to hire and train an inexperienced woman with two small children at home. I learned quickly—listed and sold a house in three weeks and was hooked. What I'm leading up to is that all my education and training were directed toward a career in teaching, and that field is still my first love. So as we talk about schools, I hope you'll excuse my putting on my teacher's hat from time to time.

I suppose we could begin by talking about the standard approach to evaluating a school system. Most books will tell you to call the school board and ask several questions. What is the average class size in the elementary school? In the secondary school? How much does the town spend per pupil? Is grouping in the elementary school homogeneous or heterogeneous? Does the high school offer vocational training? What percentage of students go on to college? What colleges?

This is all information which you should know, but it really does not tell you very much about the experience your child will have in these schools. For example, take the question, "How much does the town spend per pupil?" If the figure is high, is the extra money being spent on materials? Extra textbooks? Special programs? More experienced teachers? Athletic programs? Or highly paid administrative personnel? That dollar figure really means little unless you know where it's going and how effectively.

In reality, no person *teaches* anything *to* any other person. All education, all learning, is self-education. Knowledge and skill cannot be poured in; they must be comprehended and practiced. The function of the teacher is to guide, to show the way, to make the road easier, to help the student over the rough spots of learning. Schools and the school system provide the physical plant, the materials, the atmosphere, and, it is hoped, the impetus.

When I personally evaluate a school system, I ask: "Does it encourage *thinking* or is the emphasis on learning by rote? Which is important, getting the "right" answer or understanding? Is the emphasis on set patterns and standards to which all must conform, or is there room for special skills and talents and the encouragement to develop these skills?"

These are very elusive questions which are not easily answered by looking at statistics. Even with the help of statistics, however, the answers will always be a little different in each classroom and with each teacher. In order to understand the direction which a school system sets, we must try to get an overview, try to understand the philosophy behind the selection of new teachers and the implementation of new programs. More specifically, we can ask if there are special reading programs for the students having difficulty. Or are these students dragged along with the pack, gasping, trying always to catch up in a race that seems to gain momentum as it proceeds? We can ask if there are special classes for the gifted students, where their talents can be developed. We can ask if music and art are taught by qualified teachers and not classed as mere time fillers in the elementary school. We can ask if there is an instrumental music program, some attempt at art history, some emphasis on drama and theatre. Is there an adequate physical education program in the lower grades, or is all the money spent on high school athletics? And most important of all, we can ask, "Do the children write?" Even in the earlier grades, fill-in-the-blank teaching must be accompanied by writing which gathers information and expresses ideas. The amount and scope of this writing must increase in the upper grades, not only in the English class but in *every subject*. Only thus, through the gathering, organization, and expression of ideas, can students be taught to think for themselves.

The answers to these questions are sometimes difficult to come by. Even in the best system there will be one-word right-answer teachers, and even in the worst system there will be tell-me-what-you-think teachers. The goal is to find the system that encourages thinking, a system where teachers are hired because they have something unique to give. If you are fortunate, you may find a superintendent or administrator who will spend a few moments talking with you about the schools in which and for which he works.

Perhaps in spite of us, however, children survive in the public schools. Many go on to greater self-realization in higher education; others get caught up in the workaday world where their education is tested and greatly expanded. Before you worry unnecessarily about the "effects" of the schools upon your child, please remember that study after study has shown that the atmosphere of the home really governs the learning attitudes of the child. This is not to say that we should not seek the best we can find in a school, but only that choosing a fine school neither will nor can guarantee success, just as accepting a poor school will not predestine failure. School, formal education, is but an adjunct to what is taught in the home from early infancy. This is where attitudes and ambitions are set. The worst school and worst teachers cannot destroy the joy of life and learning in a child raised in a stimulating, encouraging home.

In addition to home and school, children also learn much from each other. The *children* with whom your children go to school will probably play as large a part in their real education as their teachers. By this I mean not only the body of knowledge to be gleaned from textbooks but also the skills for living in a community. What kind of children will your children associate with six or seven hours a day? This is of course a major question in choosing the town where you will live, and with it we come to the major question of homogeneous versus heterogeneous community.

Everyone is familiar with the upper-middle-class suburb. Well-manicured lawns, neatly painted houses, businessmen fathers, tennis-playing mothers. Carbon copies of these towns appear all across the country, usually encircling major cities. Many fine teachers actively seek jobs in them. Middle-class, stable values pervade the school system; the children are goal- and achievement-oriented, and there are usually no special discipline problems. School is a positive factor in the home, and education in the schools proceeds at a more or less quiet pace. The students graduate as the products of a middle-class world into a middle-class world.

This is of course *not* Everytown, USA, but many towns are homogeneous at one socioeconomic level or another, and there is much to be said for learning in an atmosphere of like friends. I would like to say a word in favor of the heterogeneous community, however. There can be something exciting and stimulating about attending school with persons different from yourself. It is there that one can be "schooled" in tolerance. Through contact with differing life-styles and traditions, one has an opportunity to see life through different eyes, to test his values against those of others. Most important of all, this testing can be done while the child is still a part of the protected and sheltered atmosphere of the home. It is my personal feeling that it is far better for the developing personality to come in contact with as wide a range of our society as possible while still within the supporting atmosphere of the family than for the young adult to be thrown suddenly into the heterogeneous society of the working world, or worse yet to go through the whole of life suspicious of all who are not exactly like himself.

Stacks upon stacks of books have been written on the subject of "good education," and I have barely run a finger through the dust upon them in this discussion. The magnitude of this written material itself speaks eloquently for the fact that there are no pat answers on "the schools." As with almost everything else in the House Hunt Game, *you* must decide upon your goals and your values. Get what facts you can, then talk to people who have children in the schools, talk to the kids themselves, and try to arrange a visit to a school or two in the system. While you are at the school, look about carefully, listen carefully; you will learn much.

Perhaps I have been "soapboxing" a bit on my favorite subject; in any case, it is time I put my real estate hat back on. I have talked much about evaluating the tax structure and services in a community, and this kind of careful evaluation will certainly give you a good insight into the character of the towns which you are considering. "But isn't there an easier way?" you ask. "Can't we at least eliminate *some* towns quickly?"

Well, most buyers at some point get maps and try "riding around" area towns. Contrary to popular opinion, this is *not* an easy way. It is an excellent tactic for evaluating neighborhoods within the towns you have chosen, but it just doesn't work in evaluating the towns themselves. The scope is just too large. Too much time is spent and too much gas consumed. Boredom, frustration, and often an argument over being lost set in long before any critical judgments can be made. There *are* two "quick and easy" methods for judging towns, however, and they each require a minimal expenditure of both gas and time.

To practice them you need travel only to the offices of the town zoning board and a local Realtor. The Realtor first.

A "Realtor" is a licensed real estate broker who is a member of the local real estate board, which in turn is affiliated with the National Association of Realtors. (It's a kind of professional union, as it were.) Practically all Realtors belong also to the local multiple listing service (MLS). In this way they share each other's listings, and having more houses to sell can give you better service (theoretically, anyway). The real plus for you in evaluating towns is that most MLS boards publish their listings on cards, on loose-leaf sheets, or in computer printout books. These listings contain all pertinent information on each piece of property and usually include a photo. Every real estate office I have ever been in, whether as a salesperson, customer, or guest, has arranged these listings by price, and *this* is the key to a quick and easy method of evaluating the socioeconomic character of a town. Tell the agent you are working with, or any agent you may choose as you drive down the street, that you would like to look through the listings in various towns and tell him why. As you flip the pages in his listing book, observe and/or ask, and make a note of, the *median* (not the average) sale price for houses in each town. This will tell you in what price range the largest number of houses is sold and thus give you an insight into the socioeconomic position of the majority of a town's citizens. You also want to note carefully the top and bottom prices in each town, the range of the span, and the number of listings at either extreme. This information will help you decide if a town is homogeneous or heterogeneous in nature, and to what degree.

While you are looking through listing books, talk casually with the agent about the overall atmosphere in various towns. Is this a highly mobile town (lots of corporate transfers) or one with a rather stable population? Is there a great deal of community activity or is privacy of paramount importance? Is it a commuter town; where do most of the people who live in it work? And while you're at it, don't limit this kind of conversation to real estate agents. Ask anyone with whom you can strike up a conversation how he or she feels about the town. People love to talk about the places in which they live. Some praise; some complain. You'll get a variety of opinions; but you'll see patterns begin to develop.

If a Realtor's office is the best place to get a socioeconomic overview of a town, then the zoning board office is the best place to get a physical overview. Here the evaluation tool is maps. Ask to see the current zoning maps and master plans; you will see the town past, present, and future. Note the range of lot sizes in the various residential zones. Locate the business center in the town. Where are other commercial- and industrial-zoned areas, if any? How much open space is there and how is it zoned for future development? How much park and recreation land is available currently? Will this be sufficient in ten years? Is there an area set aside in the town for future high-density housing? What about T zones? These are transition zones which were once residential and are now becoming commercial. Make special note of these, for they tend to expand slowly over the years and residential property in or near a T zone tends to diminish in value. Check and make note also of the main arteries through the town and of proposed road construction. You do not want a highway to come through or, worse yet, near your house at some future date.

The zoning office maps are X-rays of the town as it exists, and as such they are insightful and reliable. In terms of the future, however, you must not regard them as infallible. In regard to undeveloped land in particular, these maps are primarily indicators of intention on the part of the town. They are not legally binding, and the zoning can be, and rather frequently is, changed. For example, a builder may go to the zoning board with a plan for garden apartments and part of the old prestigious five-acre residential zone may be changed to a high-density area, even over the protests of the immediate neighbors. Sometimes with a major zoning change there are suspicions voiced about money changing hands under the table. This may or may not be the case; it has been my experience that most zoning board members are sincerely interested in the welfare of their communities. In any event, however, take present development as a given and the future as a maybe.

After you have narrowed your choice of towns to a workable number, you should begin evaluating neighborhoods. *Now* is the time for some serious "driving around." Neighborhood is extremely important since the houses surrounding your house will directly affect its value, present and future. The ideal situation is to own a house in the middle of a neighborhood's price range. If you buy the biggest house by far in an area, its resale value will be held down by the houses around it; if you choose the smallest house by far, its price will be raised somewhat by the value of the houses surrounding it, yet strangely enough it may not sell as quickly because its potential buyers may feel economically intimidated.

At one time "neighborhood" meant the several "blocks" around the street where one lived. In older areas this is still true. Since World War II, however, with the tremendous amount of residential building in this country, neighborhood has come to mean a builder's "development"; that is a group of homes of similar style and price range. If you choose to live in such a development, you will be choosing to live with homogeneity. The people around you will be much like yourself. For the most part, they will have similar jobs, similar incomes, and similar interests. They will want quiet streets, backyards, barbecues, "good neighbors," and a place for the children to play. To a certain extent, a development protects property value with this very sameness.

One permanently located young executive who had spent over a year looking for just the right *non*development house said to me, "If I were to be transferred to a strange city, I would tell the real estate agent to show me the highest-priced developments in the highest-priced towns that I could afford, and I would buy in one of them." Surprising? Contradictory?

Not at all. The strangeness of the city would not matter in a transfer for this man because his investment would be protected by the neighborhood he chose. He was, in fact, able to hunt down the unusual house he wanted on a quiet street of custom-built houses in this area. He succeeded partly because he thoroughly knew every town he was considering; he knew the advantages and disadvantages of every neighborhood; he had spent time in every zoning office; and he had even attended planning board meetings. He was a cautious buyer beyond all reckoning, but this very caution would have led him to buy a "tract" house in a strange city. And he would be right, for property value in a development is so inextricably tied together that even if additions and improvements are added to a property the price is *still* anchored to the neighborhood. On the other hand, even if a piece of property is allowed to become run-down in a development, it will still retain most of its value because of its area.

It is this very homogeneous interdependence which for some people is the chief *disadvantage* of the development. They are disdainful of "development people" who tend to fit certain profiles and development houses which tend to be rather interchangeable. This kind of buyer is willing to sacrifice the high sales appeal and potential quick resale of the development house for individuality, and often for increased privacy.

Many nondevelopment buyers also maintain that they are seeking quality construction. Unfortunately they may or may not achieve this goal in a custom-built house, since the quality of construction there varies as widely as that of development construction. Much depends upon the integrity of the builder and the supervision under which he worked.

To some extent development construction has earned a bad name because almost all of it is done on "spec" (speculation). The builder puts up the house as he sees fit and then sells it. Construction is supervised by neither owner nor architect, but by the builder himself. Within the same development, therefore, you will find that the quality of construction is generally consistent throughout. It may be bad, good, or indifferent, but it is generally consistent. From one development to another, however, you will find great disparity in construction quality, and price is *not* the determining factor. I've seen well-constructed lower-priced developments and poorly constructed expensive ones.

Because of builder consistency from house to house within one development, you can learn a great deal before you buy if you happen to know someone who lives in the neighborhood. Ask about construction, water problems, appliances, heat, and insulation. Even if you know no one in the whole town, however, *looking* at the other houses in a development will give you some clues to construction.

One development in the town where we now live has continued to sell at higher and higher prices each year. It is considered one of the nicer areas in town, yet its appearance is often shabby, with many of the large, elegant houses badly in need of paint. This puzzled me, and I talked to a builder friend of mine about it. "They just *can't* keep those houses looking nice," he said. "That whole tract went up like lightning several years before you came here. They were selling those houses so fast they didn't care what kind of lumber they were using, and most of it was green. The paint chips and peels because of the moisture in the wood." Sooooo, I understood. On the inside most of these houses are beautifully decorated, but if one looks carefully, he can see the floorboards pulled away from molding, cracks in the dry wall near the corners of the windows, bumps in the wall where the nails have popped. When you look at a development house, try to look at several in the same neighborhood, and look closely; the problem that is apparent in one house may just be hidden in another.

Whether you are seeking a development or a nondevelopment house, it is important that you become aware of the traffic patterns around the house before you buy. Visit the site of the property on a weekday at about 5 P.M. A house on a street that seems deserted at 2 P.M. may turn out to be on the most popular shortcut home for half the workers at the aircraft plant two miles away! While you are there, listen. Nearby traffic can be disturbing, especially in spring and summer when the windows are likely to be open. Houses which back up to, or are close to, major highways are among the most difficult to sell and *always* bring lower prices.

From my own personal experience, I must add: Never, *never* purchase anything based on the traffic which you observe on a Sunday afternoon. This traffic is always light and gives no indication of real usage. Early in our marriage, my husband and I very foolishly rented an apartment in a city completely unfamiliar to us in the quiet of a Sunday afternoon. After moving in, we discovered that we were located directly on *the* major truck route through town.

Traffic patterns can be observed (and heard), but there is another less discernible element associated with the general location of a property which must be researched. It is the question, "What was here before?" The nature and use of the land before the houses were built can tell you a lot about drainage, settling, soil type and condition, and water. Was the property farmland? Was it forest which was cleared? Where were the trees and stumps buried? Under *your* house? Was the land swampy? Sandy? Hilly? How was it filled?

Across the street from one house where we lived for only a short while was an empty lot which needed a great deal of fill. New houses were still going up in the area when we moved in, and we watched huge masses of debris from that new construction get piled into the gully near the center of the lot. About a year after we sold our house, we drove back through the development, and there sitting on top of the roots, trees, rocks, and general trash buried in that uneven lot was a raised ranch house on a level green lawn. I wouldn't take a nickel bet that the floor of that foundation would be level two years down the road. This "gully-house," as we called it, is a good example

of a property located in an excellent town, in a fine neighborhood, and on a *bad* lot.

If this location chapter could be magically dramatized, the
theatre lighting would illuminate the whole stage for the town
scenes, focus on a small group for the neighborhood scenes,
and finally encircle the hero—the residential lot. So let's turn
the spotlight now to real estate's protagonist. Lots can be dis-
tinctly individual or they can be flat pieces of earth distin-
guished from each other only by surveyor's stakes. What is
beautiful and good depends upon "the eye of the beholder."
Rational evaluations can be made, however, in terms of size,
contour of the land, and quality of the soil.

To start with size: How big is big enough? Some very lovely
and comfortable town houses are built on lots a scant forty feet
across. Yes, they are close to their neighbors, and yes, some
degree of privacy is lost. On the other hand, lawn maintenance
is minimal. Some people spend a virtual lifetime trying to
landscape and manicure three acres. They have privacy, but
they are often little more than slaves to the land.

An acre is 43,560 square feet. Most builders, however, refer
to a lot that is 200 feet by 200 feet as an acre lot. (This is 40,000
square feet.) I once sold a house on an absolutely flat two-acre
lot with not a tree in sight. As we approached the property for
the first time, it seemed to me that the For Sale sign was
standing at the edge of a green Sahara, and I'm afraid I said so.
The prospective buyer was insulted. He was most impressed
with the wide-open land, as he called it. Sometimes when I
drive by now, I see the master or his son riding around their
huge lawn on their "super deluxe" riding mower. They love it.
So, with regard to size, I must say, to each his own. Mowing
and gardening time are relevant factors, but the decision is a
personal one.

A small wooded lot can give more privacy than an expansive
circle of green, and lot *size* does not affect the value of a house
nearly as much as neighborhood. Just to give you an example,

there is a tract in the town where I now work on which executive houses in the $90,000 to $100,000 price range are built on barren hilly lots of approximately one-third of an acre. The houses are literally castles on tiny islands, but the area sells extremely well, bringing more and more money each year.

Size of lot *does* affect the value of property, however, if a small house, or indeed any kind of house, stands on a large piece of land which is zoned for smaller residential lots. In this case, after purchasing the house, the extra land around it can be broken into smaller lots (subdivided) and sold. You don't need a course in real estate principles to realize how profitable this can be. In the case of a large piece of land that *cannot* be subdivided, however, the value of the house, no matter what the price range, will be only slightly more than its value in a neighborhood of like houses on a smaller lot. After all, one building lot is still *one* building lot. The extra land produces no income, but it does add to the amount of taxes which must be paid on the property. Before you allow anyone to talk you into paying a premium price for a house because "you're getting a large piece of land with it," ask yourself what you can *do* with all the land. Do you really want it? Do you want to maintain it? Do you want to garden? Farm? Own horses? Raise dogs? Chickens? Can you sell any part of it? (The zoning board has a say in the answer to most of these questions.)

While I'm talking about size, I might as well get in a word about shape. If you were looking for a piece of sculpture for your living room, you might want something different, unique, original—*not* so with your building lot. When it comes to the shape of residential lots, normal, "ordinary," is best. Avoid zigzags, strange curves, appendages, oblique angles, wedges, pies, and interior lots connected to the road by a right-of-way. These lots are difficult to survey, often difficult to live with, and usually difficult to sell.

In some areas of this country, you have but one choice as to the contour of the land—flat. If this is your situation, you might as well skip the next few paragraphs. If, however, you are fortunate enough (or unfortunate enough, depending on your point of view) to live in a hilly area, you should be aware of what contour can mean to you.

Where roads have been put in encircling the sides of a hill, the houses are classified as "up side" and "down side," in terms of their relationship to the road. If at all possible, buy on the up side of the hill. Usually people do not mind driving up a driveway to get to a house, but they are petrified of steep driveways that go *down* toward a house. One couple I worked with had been living in such a house, where the driveway sloped steeply down with no leveling before the garage. One winter day, the wife drove down the driveway, couldn't stop because of ice, and drove right through the garage door. (She won an electric garage door opener for her prize.) It took a long time to sell this house, but the house the couple bought next was on an absolutely flat piece of land.

Flooding is another disadvantage of houses built below grade level. (Grade level is the level at which the road slopes.) Gravity dictates that rain and melting snow must go down, and the easiest path for the water to travel is often the driveway toward *your* lower-than-the-road house. In some really "low-down" houses, it is also disconcerting that people passing on the road can easily look into the second-story windows. On the other hand, buyers who choose the up side of the hill have maximum privacy in this regard.

While I'm on the subject of hills, I should mention views. Every real estate salesman in the country is an expert at selling the view. Views have an emotional appeal; they are a peg to hang a sale on. A truly beautiful one is indeed difficult to come by and worth some serious consideration, but it is only *part* of the purchase package, a part which you will seldom "use." In other words, don't "buy a view."

I must stop a moment here to tell you an amusing anecdote. For a time I was working as a saleswoman along the Connecticut shoreline. In this area homes that are oceanfront or ocean

view bring premium prices. A new listing which read "BEAU-
TIFUL VIEW OF THE OCEAN" came across my desk. The price
seemed reasonable and I quickly called a customer I had been
working with. We hurried out to see the house, thinking it
might be sold in a flash. When the listing agent met us at the
door, I was already beginning to be a bit nervous since I
couldn't "feel" the ocean nearby. We politely followed the
salesman through an ordinary house. Finally I ventured,
"Ahhhhh, this listing says, 'BEAUTIFUL VIEW OF THE OCEAN.'"
"Oh, yes," said my fellow agent, "I forgot about that." (He had
written it in capital letters on the listing form.) He took us
upstairs again to the smallest back bedroom. "Just look out this
window. See those pines over there? Well, when it's high tide,
you can see the ocean between them!"

Woods and open fields are another emotionally appealing
"sales peg." If you choose a house that is in the midst of a fully
developed area, you can be fairly certain that there will be
little major change in the future. But if you choose to live near
those appealing woods or fields, you might be on dangerous
ground unless you take the time to check very positively into
*who* owns that land.

Like most people, my husband and I find open land attractive. Our first house backed up to a woods. We loved it the
moment we saw it and never thought to ask the salesman
about the ownership of those woods. We were lucky. Perhaps
two miles further north in the town was a bluestone quarry
which had a little train running from the quarry to the main
railroad line about five miles south in the neighboring town.
The woods behind our house were a part of the right-of-way
land for that spur railroad. Four or five times a day the train
went by on a track that was nearly a mile behind our house.
Meanwhile our children played army and cowboys in those
woods, brought home a varied collection of frogs from the
shallow pond, and gathered wild raspberries each summer.
Without spending a penny or a care, we enjoyed privacy and

beauty all year round thanks to the many acres that "our" woods added to our small lot.

Choosing to be close to open land was not so auspicious in another house which we bought, however. It was located in a very small development with the streets laid out in a pattern shaped like the letter *F*. This time we did ask the agent about the open field and the distant woods at the end of the arms of the *F*. He told us that the woods belonged to a local gun club and the field to the state mental hospital. Perhaps it was wishful thinking, perhaps pure House Hunt fatigue, but we "decided" that the woods were far enough away not to be a threat, and the field would probably be a field forever. "Forever" does not exist. As I write this, the land is still open, and we are living in another house, but there have been rumblings from the state that it needs to build more housing for its employees at the hospital, and the field at the end of the *F* is being mentioned again and again as a possible location. Worse yet, when the town planning board revised its master plan, (after we had moved in) they zoned *that* field for multiple-unit housing. With the recent addition of sewers to the area, high-density housing has become a realistic possibility, the implementation of which would mean heavier traffic on the streets, more noise, and loss of privacy *and* the view. All of this would add up to diminished value for the single-family houses located in the development. So much for open land.

Last but not least on the list of emotional-appeal factors is the gurgling brook. On our first house-hunting trip to New Jersey, we were shown a lovely well-kept split-level with a bubbling brook through the backyard. I was charmed. Visions of my children wading among the rippling waters on hot summer days. Lovely idea. Unfortunately (actually very *fortunately*), we were on a reconnaissance trip at the time and were not yet in a position to buy. We let the house go, regretfully. A year later, after we were well settled elsewhere, we saw that very house on the front page of the local newspaper. Many days of spring rain had transformed the bubbling brook into a river flooding the basements of all the houses along its banks. The force of the water had also uprooted a huge tree stump and propelled it through the picture window of the basement family room in what might have been "our" house.

Besides being unpredictable at flood times, streams are often indicative of poor drainage and/or a high water table, which in turn often means a wet basement. "West-Running Brook" may be an idyllic place to write a poem in the country, but it is not desirable near the house which you must maintain.

Speaking of basements, wet ones are a major worry of most homeowners. Neither poured concrete nor cinder block (the two most commonly used foundation materials) are impervious to water. They offer some degree of resistance, it's true, but the water situation is really dependent on three factors: the quality of the soil, the level of the water table, and the grading of the lot.

Grading that gently slopes away from the house is ideal since it helps heavy rain to flow away from the foundation. Conversely, a lot which slopes toward the house is most likely to cause flooding problems. On a larger scale, try to avoid lots which are the low points or valleys of a development or neighborhood, since they too gather water from the surrounding areas.

The level of the water table is very difficult to gauge. Usually, however, high ground is less likely to have a high water table since it tends to have better drainage and is less likely to collect water. Look at as many houses as possible in a neighborhood that you are considering. Be watchful for sump pumps and try to mark on a map where the houses that have them are located. If you see a pattern developing, it is indicative of an overall problem probably related to the water table.

Type of soil is probably the most important single factor in determining the dryness of a basement. Gravel and sand tend to draw water downward quickly; clay tends to hold water. If you are about to buy in an area rural enough to have septic tanks, you will find soil type even more important, for it will determine the efficiency of the waste disposal system. Here also gravel and sand are best. You should inquire of the owner where the septic tank, dry well, and/or leach lines are located. Then go out and look at these places. Standing pools of murky water, soggy ground, and an abundance of insects are all symptoms of septic tank problems and therefore of drainage problems.

If a house is on a septic tank, the "perc" test made before it was built can tell you a great deal about soil type and drainage. A perc test (percolation test) is required by most towns before a building permit can be issued for a house that will use a septic tank in order to insure that the drainage on the land is adequate to handle waste disposal. A backhoe is brought in, a hole is dug on the property, and water is poured in. Then observations are made to determine at what rate the water drains. In the process, notations are made about the types of soil that are exposed. In most towns, perc tests are kept on file, usually in the office of the building inspector. These records are open to the public and you can request to see them. Get this information if you can, for it is a most reliable insight into drainage and soil type.

If you are looking at houses in an area lightly populated enough to have septic tanks, there is the possibility that the houses may also use well water. If you are seriously considering a house on a well, *be sure to have the water tested by a reputable laboratory before you buy.* I cannot stress this too strongly. It is so important that many banks will not give a mortgage on a house with well water without a water test. Many problems in a house can be corrected at greater or lesser expense, but poor water is an insurmountable difficulty.

When you get down to serious consideration of any one particular house, ask if the owner has a survey map of his property and, if so, ask to see it. This map will show you exactly how much land goes with the house, where the house is situated on the lot, and where the driveway, fences, and walls are located in relation to the boundaries of the lot. It will also show any easements or encroachments on the property.

An easement is essentially a right-of-way—a right to cross or use the property. Most often easements are granted to utility companies. Sewer or water lines may run along the property line or power lines above it. The easement grants the utility company access to its equipment. Another form of easement is the shared driveway, or a driveway that runs through one property to reach another. An easement is not necessarily a detriment to a property, but each instance must be evaluated individually. Usually your lawyer can be of help here.

An encroachment is some aspect of property (usually a building, fence, or wall) which intrudes upon another property. For example, your neighbor builds a doghouse for his Great Dane. When the land is surveyed, it turns out that the back half of "friend" Dane sleeps in *your* yard. The doghouse is an encroachment. If things get unfriendly, you can have the doghouse removed; the remedy is not quite so easy, however, if it is discovered that the corner of your neighbor's *garage* is actually on your property. This is why you ask to see the survey *before* you buy. If there isn't one in existence, have one done, and make your contract contingent upon the fact that the survey shows all things as they appear to be (i.e., no encroachments).

As we go on in this House Hunt Game book and these dos and don'ts, pluses and minuses begin to accumulate, you will undoubtedly have occasional moments of confusion and frustration. One house seems all pluses, but it's on a bad lot; another seems ideally located, but the floor plan is all cut up; another lot rates okay, but you simply don't *like* the house. Everything is faulted. In House Hunt, as in almost everything else, the ideal, the perfect, does not exist. What House Hunt really demands is sufficient knowledge to recognize the faults in a piece of property and sufficient self-knowledge to evaluate which faults you can best live with. So judge the location and the lot, and judge them carefully, for they are extremely important, but remember, they are *not* the only factors to be considered. Most living does actually go on *inside* the house.

# 3.

# Age, Style, and Livability

"Carolyn! You won't believe what we found!" The voice on the phone rang with the slightly shrill, artificial enthusiasm so often used to mask uneasiness. I didn't need to be told it was Jack Abbott, a buyer I had been working with almost daily for the past month; and I also didn't need to be told that he had bought a house through another sales agent.

The conversation continued:

"Good morning, Jack. What did you find?"

"You won't believe this, but we got an absolutely *brand-new* four-bedroom colonial for *only* ninety-three thousand dollars!"

I had shown them perhaps a dozen four-bedroom colonials at or near this price. But when the bell sounds, there's little sense in continuing to fight. "Really?" I said. "Where is it?"

"It's in Chatham, near the A&P."

"Huh, that's funny. I don't have any colonials listed at that price in Chatham."

"Oh, well, it's not built yet."

"Not built?"

"No, you see, Connie and I were out driving around yesterday and we saw this trailer parked near the road with a big sign on it that said, 'New Homes. Come in and inspect our original floor plans.' So we thought we'd go in just to get some ideas. Well, it turned out that this builder is just opening up this beautiful development, and we had a chance to get in on the ground floor. There were only two other lots sold, so we had a great choice, and we saved money too 'cause all the prices on all the models are going up two thousand dollars after they make the cuts for the roads."

His voice was running away with excitement.

"You mean you didn't actually see your lot?" I asked.

"Well, we walked around on the property, but it was kind of muddy and hard to tell where we were on the map. But they will have it all staked out in a month or so."

I had a sick-at-heart feeling for this young first-home buyer. He was an intelligent junior executive but obviously an innocent babe in the buying game.

"Did you sign a contract or leave a deposit?" I asked.

"Yeah, we only had to give a down payment of three thousand dollars. Wasn't that great? Then we'll put five thousand more down when they actually begin construction on our house."

I politely congratulated him, accepted his very sincere thanks for my time and efforts in trying to find them a house, and wished them well. There was nothing else I could do.

I cannot think of a worse way to buy a house. This couple actually paid out three thousand dollars of their savings for a promise. They did not see the actual site upon which the promise would be constructed, and they knew nothing about the quality of that construction. After looking at some appealing pictures and floor plans, they got caught up in the enthusiasm of the moment and actually signed the builder's contract without consulting their own attorney. At best, they will get a new house something like their dream somewhere near the date it was promised; at worst, they will lose their three thousand dollars. In either case, they have many days of emotional strain ahead of them, for there will most certainly be myriad problems.

The Abbotts were captured by the emotional trap of newness. The dream of having everything sparkling clean and "just the way we want it" is the motivating factor for many new-home sales. This is especially apparent on tracts where

agents sit every weekend monitoring "open houses." The buying couple falls in love with the model, which the agent carefully explains is not for sale, and then proceeds to promise and
sell *exactly* the same house on a lot "just down the road."

Buying such a "paper" house after seeing the tract model
homes is almost as risky a way to buy as the Abbotts' absolutely blind method. The model home you inspect is usually
built and decorated with care. Lighting fixtures, floor coverings, hardware, plumbing fixtures, and cabinetry are invariably the best available through that particular builder, and
selection of identical items usually adds extra dollars to the list
price of the paper house. In construction of a house, there is
also considerable latitude in the quality of materials and
workmanship, and it is difficult, if not impossible, to be certain
that the house to be built will be truly comparable to the
model. Remember therefore that even though the model provides you with a sample of the builder's work, that sample is
*not* the house which you will own.

If you are determined to proceed on a builder's promise, the
most important thing you can do is to contact an attorney who
has had extensive experience working with builders. Have
him write the most detailed and specific contract that he can,
paying particular attention to building specifications, comple-
tion dates, and construction guarantees, with stiff and specific
penalties for failure to comply.

Beyond building it yourself, working with an architect, or
buying a builder's paper house, you have two choices in the
House Hunt Game: new or resale. By "new" I mean a house
which the builder has built on spec, a house essentially complete, which you can inspect before you buy. Model homes
can fall into this category if you buy the model itself, *and* they
can be excellent buys.

If you are considering the purchase of a model, however, be
slightly wary of the overdecorated house. Carpet, wallpaper,
and draperies may be employed to mask such flaws as cracks

in the wallboard, popped nails, warped floorboards, or worse. One model home which I know of had an improperly poured concrete slab under the family room. During the particularly hard winter in which the house was for sale, the floor in that family room cracked and heaved. This in turn caused some serious cracks in the walls. When I stopped by the house again in the spring, however, I was amazed to see thickly padded carpet on the family room floor and beautiful paneling on the walls. The effect was elegant and the faults could not be seen. This, of course, is an extreme case, but look behind the draperies and under the carpets if you can. If everything seems to be in order, the extra amenities of the model can add considerably to the value of your purchase and at the same time save precious out-of-pocket dollars.

It is the lack of extras and amenities which is one of the major disadvantages in buying new, particularly if you are "cutting it close" money-wise. Landscaping, storm windows, screens, doorstops, a mailbox, curtain rods, shades, light bulbs, carpeting, and some appliances are usually left behind by the previous owner in a resale, but all must be purchased and paid for separately in a new house.

Firm price is another disadvantage of buying new. Most builders figure their profit closely, and only rarely and under pressure are they willing to negotiate even small reductions in price. Even real estate commissions are considerably lower on new houses. Essentially, therefore, you must assume that the new house will cost you *more* than the price you see listed, for you will have to pay that list price and the out-of-pocket cost of necessary extras. On the other hand, the resale house usually includes the extras *and* almost always has room in the price for negotiation.

One advantage of a new house, however, is that it usually provides greater appreciation on your money, especially in the first few years after purchase. Once a development is complete and the homeowners begin to add distinctive personal touches to the houses and landscaping, there is usually a substantial jump in values, notably higher than the overall appreciation in housing due to inflation.

There is one very specialized situation in the large incomplete development which especially beckons to value-conscious buyers, for it can offer all the advantages of a new house with few or none of the disadvantages. As you drive through the tract, be on the lookout for houses which are up for resale. In tract sales, the price of the models tends to set a ceiling on house prices throughout the development. Despite the fact that a family might have spent several thousand dollars on landscaping, carpets, decorating, and finishing touches, their house will not sell appreciably higher than that model home down the street. So if you should see a broker's For Sale sign or a For Sale By Owner sign while you are in "Happy Acres Estates," be sure to stop and take down the phone number. Then inspect the models and take careful note of exactly what is included in the price. If you like what you see there, by all means inspect the resale house.

If price and/or availability put new construction out of the question for you, or if you prefer not to hassle with the problems of newness, you still have the greater bulk of the real estate market left to choose from. The range and variety of resale houses is enormous; from run-down "handyman specials" to Victorian gingerbread mansions without plumbing, from well-maintained vine-covered cottages to the ten-month-old custom-built being sold by a transferred executive. After all, houses are the homes of people and they reflect therefore the tremendous variety of human tastes and interests.

The major advantage in all resales is that you can see exactly what you are buying. Potential problems such as severe settling, green lumber, inadequate septic systems, wet basements, etc., have usually materialized and manifested themselves. Of course, there has also been time for the creative homeowner to attempt to mask these problems, but a watchful eye and a thorough inspection can usually turn up clues which will lead to their discovery. (But I'll discuss trouble-spot sleuthing in the next chapter.)

The major disadvantage of the resale is age related: the need for redecorating, cleaning, and maintenance work. All the working equipment in a resale has been in use, and its likelihood of breakdown is roughly proportional to its age and probable life span. So the resale disadvantage of redecorating and potential repairs somewhat balances the new-house disadvantage of extra expenses, the difference being, however, that new-house extra costs are obvious and immediate demands for out-of-pocket cash, whereas the maintenance costs in a resale are something of an unknown which may or may not make demands on reserve cash supply.

Houses under five years old can be considered new in terms of potential maintenance problems. In fact, between one and five is probably the optimum age at which to buy a house. The builder has usually remedied his errors and solved his problems by the end of that first year or so of battle with the first owner. Also, by the end of a year, settling or warping, popped nails due to green lumber, and wet basements are usually apparent. Thus, in the case of the almost-new resale, you can see exactly what you are buying, many of the finishing touches and extras have already been added and paid for, *and* you can be relatively certain of minimal maintenance costs.

In houses between five and twenty-five years old, much depends upon the maintenance, care, and attention which the house has received from its owners. If you are considering a house within this age span, try to ascertain how many owners there have been. The fewer the better. People who stay in a house for a long period of time tend to maintain it more carefully, since they are maintaining it for themselves. Often, people moving in and out for short periods of time leave the problems for the next guy.

In older houses, by which I mean everything from completely renovated Revolutionary War landmarks to pre–World War II structures, you must look closely at what "has been done." Like the beautiful walnut rocking chair with seven coats of different-colored paint on it, older houses have been modified and remodified to suit the tastes and life-styles of their numerous owners. In the process, much has been covered over, sometimes for the better, sometimes for the worse.

Friends of ours in an older custom-built house have a beautiful and romantic alcove in their living room which holds a splendid fireplace of white brick with built-in bookshelves and bench seats on either side. One evening we were sharing with them information about one of our "great places to get firewood" and were astounded when they said that the fireplace was artificial. Once indeed a working fireplace, the former owners had closed it off and were proud of their artificial replacement.

In such a way are plaster walls boarded over with simulated wood paneling, artistic ceilings transformed by suspended acoustical tile, stained glass windows replaced, and ceramic tile covered over with Formica. When inspecting older houses, ask tactfully about the "improvements" and additions.

The age of a house appears somewhere near the top of the page on practically every type of listing sheet I have seen. The entries there are usually accurate since there is little one can do to be "creative" with numbers. Adjacent to the space for age, however, is usually a category headed "Style" where accuracy is not always of primary importance. The entry under style is sometimes a sales come-on, the first on the page. Do not regard it as a *reliable* indication of appearance or floor plan. Despite the latitude used by real estate salesmen in filling in this category, however, certain terms have come to represent, at least generally, certain types of houses. The following list therefore is essentially a vocabulary lesson.

*Older:* This can mean anything from a Victorian castle without plumbing to a run-down Quonset hut to a well-maintained 1930s town house. Most often it is attached to architecturally nondescript houses, usually in need of repair and remodeling. If you see the term "older" on a listing, look carefully at the photo of the house for clues to its condition, or better yet, ask the agent if he has seen it.

*Two-Story:* This is a variation of "older." It is rarely applied to tasteful, stylish homes and might well be translated "unimpressive" or "nondescript." The term is rarely applied to two-family houses.

*Town House:* These can be quite old or brand-new. The term generally connotes a house of two or three stories on a rather narrow lot relatively near the center of town. As opposed to "older" and "two-story," it usually indicates a well-maintained and tastefully decorated piece of property. When applied to new construction, "town house" usually indicates high-density housing, often attached three- or four-unit buildings with garages under. Very often these are condominiums.

*Cape Cod:* This term generally indicates a small house, although this is not necessarily the case. The name evolved from a type of house popular in the Cape Cod area in which the upstairs bedrooms are directly under the pitched roof and therefore have pitched ceilings and dormer windows. The style was widely built in the post–World War II boom since it provided relatively inexpensive housing with potential expansion possibilities for the large number of young families seeking to buy. The basic plan is a four-room design: two bedrooms, one bath, living room, and kitchen. There is usually a center hall with a staircase leading to the attic. This attic area may or may not have been finished into bedrooms with or without an extra bath. Being directly under the roof, the upstairs bedrooms tend to be warm in the summer and cold in the winter, regardless of the quality of the insulation. In "Capes" in which the upstairs has been finished, one of the downstairs bedrooms has often been converted into a dining room.

Capes can be charming homes, particularly for the small family that wants extra guest rooms. The style as it was popular in the forties, however, has lost much of its appeal, and these small houses are often rather difficult to sell.

*Ranch:* This term designates a one-story house, nothing more. There is a huge range of price and style within this category, from the very cheapest bungalow to the most expensive sprawling contemporary. The variety of floor plans and traffic patterns is tremendous, but all ranches do have a few common features. Excepting those built on slabs, ranches have relatively large basements which, if dry, provide excellent storage, playroom, and workshop area. They are also slightly more expensive to heat because of the larger exposed surface area. They may or may not have garages, which may be under the house or attached, either directly or by a "breezeway." The lack of stairs makes them popular with both young families and older people. A well-maintained ranch with a good traffic pattern generally has excellent resale value since the one-story house is still extremely popular and sought after.

*Raised Ranch or Bi-level:* As the TV set became as widespread a "necessity" as the telephone, the idea of a casual, comfortable room for viewing, separate from the more formal living room, took on great popularity. In order to provide this room without further expanding the size of their foundations, builders began to build the "raised ranch." The entrance to these houses is between floors, with half a flight of stairs going up and half a flight going down. On the upper floor, the traffic pattern is essentially that of a standard ranch of the sixties: bedrooms on one side of the house, living room, dining area, and kitchen on the other. On the lower level are the family room, laundry facilities, furnace room, storage room, usually a half bath, sometimes an extra bedroom, and the garage. (Occasionally a raised ranch will have an attached garage.) By definition this style does *not* have a basement. The plan has the advantage of providing much usable living area for the dollar, but it has several disadvantages. The front entrance stairway causes awkwardness in welcoming and bidding farewell to guests because of the small foyer between floors. Many young families also object to the rather distinct separation of family room and kitchen by these stairs, and their location creates a stressful traffic pattern through the formal living room area, usually over the most expensive carpeting in the house. Another disadvantage is the limited storage area created by the lack of a basement, which also sometimes makes for difficulty in heating the lower level. Those raised ranches which have "radiant heat," that is, circulating hot water with coils embedded in the foundation floor, are warm and comfortable, however.

Raised ranches, or bi-levels, are not generally among the best-selling houses on the books; however, they do have appeal for people looking for maximum space for the dollar. If you are considering this style, you should be aware of its disadvantages and weigh them against price and extra space. You should also look with special care at the lot upon which the house is built, for bi-levels, having no basement, are sometimes constructed on problem lots where there is poor drainage or rock which would require blasting.

*Expanded Ranch:* This is usually a larger and rather elegant version of the Cape Cod. Since the term "Cape" connotes the postwar row house to many people, developers and real estate agents hesitate to use it to describe these larger, newer, and more expensive houses; hence the term "expanded ranch." The floor plan of the main level is that of a ranch with varying degrees of modification. Sometimes one, two, or even three bedrooms are located on this main level. The single feature which all expanded ranches have in common is the entry foyer with a formal stairway to the attic. This attic area may or may not be finished into additional bedrooms and baths. These rooms on the upper level usually have at least partially pitched ceilings and dormer windows. There is almost always a large basement for storage, and garages are either attached or under.

*Split Level:* This was the favorite floor plan of the fifties and is still being commonly built. The basic plan is on three levels: the living room, dining room or dining area, and kitchen form the main level; from this, usually at the central core of the house, there is a split staircase, half a flight of stairs going to the upper level and half to the lower. Bedrooms and bath(s) are generally on the upper level, and family room, half bath, and/or laundry room are generally on the lower level. Some splits have a fourth basement level beneath the living room–dining area–kitchen which provides much-needed storage space. Garages are usually under the bedroom part of the house adjacent to the family room, although in some newer and larger models the garage is attached. Split levels sell relatively well, especially to middle-income families. Their floor plan and traffic pattern is generally considered superior to the raised ranch since people can move from one level to another without passing through the formal living room area and since the kitchen is generally in close proximity to the family room.

*Front-to-Back Split Level:* This is a variation of the standard side-to-side split which never really caught on, although I have seen scattered examples of it in many areas. In these houses, the living room, dining area, and kitchen are stretched across the front of the house. The split stairway is located in the center of the house, usually at the end of the inside wall at the back of the living room. The living room and dining area share a one-and-a-half-story ceiling which extends up under the roof and which is most often complimented by the name "cathedral ceiling." The roof at the back of the house is raised approximately a half-story so that the bedrooms on the upper level do *not* have dormer windows. The family room, laundry room, and furnace and storage areas are located on the lower level under the bedrooms. There is usually a crawl space under the living room–dining area–kitchen, but no basement as such. If there is a garage, it is generally attached at the kitchen end of the house.

The front-to-back split has the disadvantages of several different styles of housing. It lacks storage facilities; it is difficult to heat because of the living areas directly under the roof and the location of the family room on a slab; and there is heavy

traffic between family room and both the kitchen and the bedrooms over the central stairway and therefore *through* the living room and dining area.

*Tudor:* Popular in the twenties and thirties, this is a style
which is reminiscent of English Tudor architecture. Pre–
World War II Tudors were generally built of stone or brick and
are characterized by rooms which jut out from the "normal"
rectangular shape of the house and by half levels within the
house. They have a rather distinctive front foyer which usually
has a decorative doorway with a separate curved and extended
roof. These lovely and graceful houses are most often found on
established city streets and are usually elegant, large, and
well-maintained properties. The term "Tudor" has become
popular again in the seventies, especially for larger new
construction. The seventies' version usually features an
authentic-looking beam and stucco facade; however, most in-
teriors have a rather common rectangular two-story floor plan.

*Colonial:* This is the favorite of the seventies. "Colonial" is
probably the most common term used to describe new two-
story construction. These houses are generally in the upper
price group. They have three to five bedrooms and two full
baths on the upper level, and a living room, formal dining
room, eat-in kitchen, lavatory, family room, and sometimes a
study or maid's quarters on the main level. They almost always have a basement and a two-car garage which may be
either attached or under. Variations which you see noted on the
listing forms, such as Dutch colonial, French provincial, and
Southern colonial, usually refer to differences in the appearance of the facade only and rarely affect the design and traffic
pattern of the interior.

Currently, colonial is the most often requested style in housing. Because of its popularity, many real estate salesmen des-
ignate any relatively presentable two-story house as a colonial,
so be skeptical of newspaper ads promising colonials at bargain prices.

*Contemporary:* This is a catch-all term which merely indicates modern styling. The house may be an architect-designed multilevel creation or a raised ranch with large windows.

So much for style; but style and livability do not necessarily go hand in hand. What may be aesthetically appealing to the members of a particular family may not fit their life-style. Each stage of life seems to have its distinctive needs, and within those stages, each individual family, and indeed each individual, has distinctive habits and preferences. Distinctive needs, habits, and preferences, three human elements which explain why houses are different from each other. And in order to choose successfully among those different houses, you must be aware of your own needs, habits, and preferences. In order to help you to formulate and clarify these for yourself and your family, let's survey general buyer attitudes toward various aspects of housing. What follows is a collection of my observations as I have watched people "look."

Traffic pattern, the way people move through a house in the course of their daily lives, is probably the single most important factor in determining a family's happiness and comfort in a house. Poor traffic pattern can mean worn-out carpets, extra floor cleaning, many extra steps each day, and a kind of getting in each other's way which is different from lack of privacy.

In evaluating traffic patterns, the most important clues are entranceways, hallways, and stairs. Look first at the entranceways, beginning with the front. Is there a foyer or greeting area? Few people like to walk directly into the living room. This foyer is most serviceable if the floor is of tile, slate, or other easily cleaned material which will withstand heavy wear.

The "best" back door is one which opens into a laundry or utility room where coats and boots can be removed and mud, dust, and sand shaken from the children's clothing and the dog's feet. The best alternative to a back entry room is entry through the garage, since this also provides a somewhat sheltered place to remove outerwear and accumulated dirt. Back entranceways directly into the kitchen or family room can bring outdoor dirt in and cause crowding and clutter as coats are being removed. These kitchen doors, however, are superior to a trend which I have observed in many new houses, where the only means of getting from the back of the house to the backyard is through the sliding glass doors of the family room. This is the worst possible arrangement for a family with small children. The sliders are essentially unusable in winter since they allow massive amounts of cold air to flow in as the children laboriously open and close them. Summer also poses a problem since the doors require both glass and screens. Children are known for their ability to leave these screens ajar, a situation that usually goes unnoticed until the flies begin to gather around the strawberry shortcake.

In houses of more than one story, the location of the stairs, particularly in relation to the kitchen and family room, gives the best indication of traffic flow. When you look at a house, trace the walking patterns from family room to kitchen and family room to bedrooms. Ideally the path should not pass through the formal living or dining rooms or through the working area of the kitchen.

It is difficult to be creative with hallways; they are simply a necessity, a means of getting from one place to another. Most people find especially long ones unappealing, however. We made the mistake of buying a four-bedroom ranch with a hallway which we later nicknamed "the bowling alley." Despite the fact that I insisted on painting it creamy yellow with a yellow, gold, and white shag carpet on the floor, it always seemed dark and closed.

No matter how long or dark, however, a hallway is preferable to a walk-through room. I remember one five-bedroom colonial which I showed to a particularly large number of buyers. The house was almost new, fairly priced, in a good neighborhood, and nicely decorated. It didn't sell for almost a year. The reason? Every family to whom I showed it had essentially the same comment, "Why did they put one bedroom

between two others?" In that house, the only access to the
fifth bedroom was through one of the two adjoining it. The
builder had conceived of it as a playroom between the rooms
of two young children or later as a study room for older children, but the response to it was almost universally negative.

Another house which I know well has the kitchen located at one end with the only access to the rest of the house
*through* the dining room. This essentially means that the dining room doubles as a hallway.

The exception to the walk-through-room taboo is, of course,
the kitchen, which is so often located in the center of the
house. This exception is valid, however, only if the walk-
through path does not interfere with the actual working area.

Another important element in traffic flow is the relationship
of bathrooms to bedrooms and main living area. One of the
most difficult houses to sell is the two-story pre–World War II
house which has only one bathroom, located on the second
floor. Buyers universally look for a conveniently located lavatory on the main floor of a house.

One last point about traffic patterns: Imagine yourself bringing groceries into the house. Is there a convenient step-saving
path? Especially inconvenient in this respect is any style with
the garage under it. One must walk up a full flight of stairs
with every bag in order to get the week's purchases from the
car to the kitchen.

Although traffic pattern is the most important factor in determining general livability, it is usually the kitchen which
sells or holds back a house. This is the room most full of sales
pegs, and "eat-in" is the feature most in demand. In order to
sell a house quickly and profitably today, it is almost essential
that it have a casual eating area either in or adjacent to the
kitchen. A breakfast bar with stools is often sufficient, as long
as there is a place to have a cup of coffee in the kitchen.

I don't think it necessary to discuss in detail all the desir-
ables of a kitchen, since they are pretty much universal:
cabinets—plenty of them; a pantry, if possible—these have

regained popularity in the seventies; built-ins—range, oven, dishwasher, disposal; counter space—seven feet of unbroken work area is ideal, but seldom found; and enough elbow room for two or more people to work without tripping over one another. "Newness" is another major selling point, along with sunlight and "cheer."

Next to "Is there an eat-in kitchen?" I most often hear, "How many bathrooms does it have?" Everyone wants at least one and a half, although this is difficult to come by in older and smaller houses. Location is also important. There should be one in or near the bedroom area and at least a lavatory near the family room. Without these, the house will be more difficult to sell and will bring less money.

Bathroom fixtures, like kitchen appliances, are most indicative of the age of a house, and old or poorly maintained ones often turn people away. On the other hand, a remodeled bathroom can be an attractive selling point. Among the most desirable bathroom features is the walk-in shower stall which a great many prefer to the shower-over-tub arrangement.

Bathroom lighting and ventilation is seldom noticed by buyers as they tour a house, yet it is unquestionably important. In newer construction, it is now common to build interior bathrooms, that is, bathrooms with no window to the outside. Local building codes require that these interior bathrooms have some kind of ventilating system. Some of these systems turn on automatically with the light switch, producing a constant whir which many buyers find annoying; other systems can be controlled independently of the lights. Generally it is preferable to have windows in all the bathrooms to provide both light and fresh air; however, buyer objection to interior bathrooms is not particularly strong.

Bedrooms are so important in house selection that they are used as a classification tool; you will hear agents refer to a house as a two-bedroom, a five-bedroom, etc. Four is the number currently in vogue, but in the fifties, it was three. Two-bedroom houses are generally quite difficult to sell, and five bedrooms are difficult to find. Some families, generally those with young children, prefer that all the bedrooms be located close together; others prefer a separate master bedroom area. Everyone, of course, checks closet space. (His and hers walk-in closets in the master bedroom are another innovation of the seventies which has become popular on everyone's dream list.)

Speaking of closets, check to be sure that the house which you are considering has adequate linen closet space, a utility closet downstairs near the kitchen, and a guest closet in the foyer or near the front door. People often forget to look for these obviously necessary storage areas, and it is surprising how very many houses in all price ranges lack them.

There are two schools of thought on living rooms. One opts for large and formal, the other for small and intimate. Both styles sell well as long as they are separate from the main activity areas of the house.

In regard to dining rooms, there is a definite preference for the separate room over the dining "L" or dining area off the living room. "Ls" are generally found in smaller houses, however, and they do offer the advantage of allowing a party to spill over into the living room, if necessary.

Family rooms: everyone wants one. Size and location can vary greatly, and both are important in influencing the sale of a house. Generally speaking, the larger the family room and the closer to the kitchen, the better. In older houses, owners have often converted other rooms into family rooms, sometimes very tastefully. In smaller houses, you will see family rooms which have been added on, with varying degrees of success. Least popular among buyers is the do-it-yourself basement family room; however, this is still preferable to no family room at all.

Most buyers want a fireplace; some want two, one in the living room and one in the family room. I can't say which sells better, living room or family room. It's really pretty much a matter of personal taste. Although good sales pegs when they are present in a house, fireplaces are usually on people's "we would like to have" lists rather than their "we must have" lists.

In most parts of the country, garages are a highly desirable feature, and many buyers will not even look at a house without one. The two-car garage has become a standard part of larger new construction; lower-priced houses, however, usually have only one. The detached garage is the least popular with house buyers since it is often too small for station wagons and larger cars and becomes essentially a storage shed. Garages which are under the house do not seem to deter buyers at all, yet it has been my experience that this arrangement can often mean colder rooms above the garage area.

When you look at a garage, try to gauge its size. It is best, but often difficult, to see it both with cars and empty. Observe how much space remains to move around the cars when they are inside. Can both driver and passengers get out? Is there storage space for the outside equipment (bicycles, lawn mowers, kiddy pools, rakes, shovels, etc.) that travels with every family?

Attics and basements, although not considered living areas, definitely figure into the livability *and* salability of a house. In many parts of the country, there is tremendous buyer resistance to houses without basements. Better heating and insulation are helping to dispel this reluctance to buy, but basement advocates will list storage space and hobby and workshop areas high on their list of needs.

Some people in houses without basements effectively use attic storage. In older houses, this is quite satisfactory since many have permanent stairways to the floored attic. The least desirable attic access is through the trapdoor in a bedroom closet, since the small opening is both difficult to negotiate and limiting. Functional, space saving, and most common in newer houses is the pull-down stairway.

Optimally, basements should have entranceways from both inside and outside the house. A metal hatch door is the most common arrangement for outside access when the basement floor is entirely below ground level. On sloping lots, many basements have walkout doors or access through the garage under the house. If there is only one access to the basement, however, it is preferable that it be through the inside of the house.

Before we leave the interior of the house, I'd like to give a passing nod to the subject of additions since you will probably see at least one "added-to" house somewhere along the way. Over the years, several friends who know that I work in real estate have asked me for my opinion on whether they should add on to their present house or buy a larger house for their expanding families. This is a difficult question to answer. Adding on avoids the disruption of family life inherent in selling and buying. It also allows the owners to maintain their current mortgage payment and interest rate. Homeowners who add on, however, rarely get the cost of the additions back in appreciation; first, because the surrounding houses usually hold the price down no matter what the addition cost, and second, because it is very difficult to make an addition "feel natural." The potential buyers sense the added-on quality in the walk-through rooms, extra-long hallways, or unaccountable turns and bends in the floor plan.

If you are enchanted with an added-to house, and if the traffic pattern is not uncomfortable for you, you may get a great deal of living space for your money. Do not, however, buy under the illusion that you are getting a "super bargain." Many buyers get caught up in a numbers game. They reason: "The houses on this street which are just like this one but do not have the addition are selling for sixty thousand. This addition cost nine thousand. The sellers are anxious and we can probably buy the house for sixty-three thousand. When we sell in five or six years, we'll make a fortune!" Not so. You *are* getting a bargain in extra living space which you are not paying full price for, but five or six years from purchase, you will probably sell that house for three or four thousand dollars more than the other houses in the neighborhood are then selling for, just as when you bought it. There is much buyer resistance to additions, and added-to houses rarely sell quickly or at good prices.

If you are intent upon buying a house with an addition, be extra careful to check the workmanship in the "adding-on." Look also for cracks in the foundation, since an improperly time in the attic looking for signs of water seepage where the roof was joined. If you can get up on top of the roof, look for signs of shingles which were patched or are pulling away. Look also for cracks in the foundation, since an improperly constructed addition can put stress on the structural soundness of the house.

One couple I know put a $20,000 family room addition, complete with a massive floor-to-ceiling fieldstone fireplace, onto their $80,000 home. Within six months, the addition was pulling away from the house and they were suing the builders. It was a very difficult house to sell somewhat later, even after the repairs had been done. (One can't help but wonder if those repairs are permanent!)

Leaving or entering a house, you will undoubtedly notice the landscaping. For some people, landscaping is an important part of livability; others want only the smallest amount of grass to cut once a week. This is, of course, a decision which each family makes individually; let me say, however, that if you buy a house in need of complete relandscaping, or a new house with three shrubs planted in front and twelve handfuls of grass seed cast on the topsoil, it will cost you both time and money in abundance.

It is very difficult for most people to remain detached and cool when house hunting, and very few buyers base their choices upon rational evaluations. Many get caught up in appearances and decorating and buy a house which looks lovely but just doesn't work for them. In order to avoid this major error, try a house out mentally. Have each person in the family imagine his way through a typical day in the house. Where would you most likely come in after work? Where would you hang your coat? Where would you read the newspaper? Who would use the showers in the morning? At night? Imagine cooking breakfast, doing the laundry, folding clothes, ironing, bringing in the groceries. Think your way through an evening entertaining dinner guests or having a large party. What are your hobbies? Will you be able to enjoy them without interfering with others? Have each person in the family write out the pluses and minuses that occur to him as he "lives through" a day in the house. Then compare notes. You will look at the house more rationally, and you will be less influenced by the beautiful draperies, the massive fireplace, or the marvelous view.

# 4.

# Looking for Trouble Spots

All specialists have special interests. One doctor might be superb in treating heart and lung ailments; another may find arthritis a fascinating disease and be right on top of the latest research in the field. Both, however, hang out their shingles as specialists in internal medicine.

Now I don't presume to compare selling real estate with the lofty practice of medicine, but I too am a specialist with a specialty. My experience in the real estate profession has been confined to residential property and my special interest is people. In the game this specialty means matching houses to buyers on a one-to-one basis, and after making the "match," arranging the details of the "wedding"—negotiating the price, getting the mortgage, and arranging for the closing.

As a House Hunt Game Coach I feel obliged at this point, however, to qualify my qualifications, especially since I'm about to embark upon a chapter on the construction, condition, and maintenance of the houses you will be looking at. I have never built a house. When I must use a hammer, I invariably bang my thumb. One grade of lumber looks much like another to me, and standards of roofing tiles, insulation, plumbing materials, etc., are about as familiar to me as the molecular charts we studied in high school chemistry.

"How can this woman possibly write a chapter on house construction and condition?" you ask.

Don't think for a moment that I haven't asked myself the same question. Rummaging about in some traditional how-to-buy-houses books, I found an easy solution to the problem. Most writers peppered their construction and maintenance chapters with, "Get an expert opinion . . . expert opinion . . . expert opinion . . . expert opinion . . ." This is advice which can't lose; the writer is safe—the question is someone else's responsibility. If, however, for every house in which you have an interest you hire an electrician, a plumber, a mason, a carpenter, a roofer, a tile man, and a landscape architect, you won't have enough cash left for the down payment. Better you should be able to spot major problems on your own and make judgments based upon your knowledge. Save the "expert opinion" for a questionable item or two in that house which you are about to buy.

Keeping in mind therefore that I promised to give you the benefit of my experience, I'll put my head upon the block, as it were, and proceed with a chapter on construction and condition. I am married to an electrical engineer, a dyed-in-the-wool do-it-yourselfer; and I am a dyed-in-the-wool observer, question-asker, and reader. Along the way, the two of us have picked up a fair amount of disjointed knowledge about houses. It is this knowledge and experience that I can share with you.

Shall we start at the bottom? The basement is literally and figuratively the foundation of the house and, as such, it may determine the success or failure of your choice.

The first thing everyone looks for is water. (Wet basements and termites are the house buyer's greatest fears.) In my several years of house exploring, I have seen some ingenious ways of trying to hide a water problem in the basement. People take out the light bulbs where the sump pump is located and then pile odd storage pieces around. I have seen handsome upholstered bench seats built over sump pumps, and I have seen laundry strung over lines across the basement, making it virtually impossible to inspect carefully.

The presence of a sump pump, however, does not necessarily mean trouble. Sometimes, especially in developments situated on low-lying land, the pump is installed when the house is built as a preventative measure. It costs less for the builder to install it while construction is in progress than to return to install it at the demand of an irate buyer. Many houses with sump pumps in the basement will have a water problem only in the event of exceptionally heavy rains, perhaps once or twice a year. In these cases, the sump pump can, and usually does, prevent a flooded basement. That pump may sit silent for months and the sudden sound of its motor starting up on a rainy night might awaken you from a comfortable sleep. But anyone who has gone down to his basement during a downpour, or perhaps returned from a vacation after several days of rain and found everything floating about, will welcome that awakening at the sound of the sump pump motor. You want to avoid, however, the house in which the pump must work more or less constantly just to keep even. This situation is indicative of major trouble. A water problem which keeps the pump that busy is likely to cause structural damage to the foundation, to say nothing of the fact that the problem itself could become unmanageable in times of exceptionally heavy rain or in the event of electrical power failure or mechanical breakdown.

If there is a sump pump in the basement, try to talk with the owners or ask your salesman to talk with them. Ask how often it runs. Ideally visit the house on a rainy day or after an early spring thaw and listen for it to turn on. If you are acquainted with anyone in the area, ask him specifically how often his pump runs. *Avoid* houses in an area where pumps must run every day, even if you *love* the house and the price seems to beckon. Every rainstorm will strain your love with worry, and the pump's contribution to your electric bill will be a monthly reminder of loving "not wisely but too well."

Sump pump or no sump pump, however, check for other signs of a wet basement: dark stains on the walls or floor, flaking plaster or paint on the walls, or a thin white line (the high-water mark) at an even level all around the basement. If you do suspect wetness, you absolutely must speak with the owner. Ask him, "Do you get water in your basement?" Make the question just that direct and explicit, and if possible, do it in front of an uninvolved witness—the salesman will do. Or have the salesman ask, but be sure to confirm what he tells you: "You mean Mr. Seller says he has *never* had any water in his basement?"

Explicit, direct answers are extremely important here. At one time the law turned its back on the house buyer. The courts essentially said, "Let the buyer beware." In fact, most preprinted real estate contracts still contain paragraphs saying that the seller makes no representation as to the quality or structural soundness of the house, and the buyer accepts what he sees. These paragraphs, however, can be rewritten, altered, or struck out by a competent attorney. Clauses such as "except that the seller represents that water has not seeped through the walls of the basement during the term of his ownership" or "the seller represents the basement to be dry" can be added. The courts have now become much more stringent on matters of false representation in real estate and several buyers have won suits for hidden defects.

Some wet basements can be repaired by regrading outside the house and installing better downspouts and gutters in order to take the water away from the foundation. This is a relatively minor project which can often be done at a small cost. Other wet basements need professional waterproofing and major structural repairs, which can run into huge expenditures. If you absolutely *must* have a particular house and you suspect a water problem, you need *several* professional estimates as to the extent and cost of the work which should be done. If you get three separate estimates and they all more or less agree on procedures and price, you can be fairly sure that the evaluation is accurate. If the estimates and evaluations differ, however, either one of the companies is out to make some extra money or the problem is an uncertain one—which means the solution may also be uncertain.

This procedure of getting three or more estimates for any

type of repair or remodeling work is always advisable, but especially so in the case of wet basements. The house cannot be moved off that foundation and the problem therefore cannot be entirely visualized. Much depends upon the knowledge, experience, competence, and honesty of the person doing the evaluation. No homeowner wants to pay for an expensive waterproofing job when regrading and better downspouts would have solved the problem. All of which boils down to: if you are determined to go ahead on a "wet" house, proceed with *great* care.

I mentioned a while ago some devices for hiding sump pumps, but I didn't say that if you climb through and over annoying storables and laundry in the basement of a house and find that they do *not* hide a sump pump, the house probably doesn't need one. That very untidy clutter which is so unappealing to the eye is one of your best guarantees that the basement is dry. No homeowner is likely to leave his possessions directly on a basement floor which might be flooded over without warning. I am much more suspicious of an overly clean basement.

On one of our house hunts, my husband and I were very much impressed with a beautifully maintained and decorated ranch in a prime neighborhood. We were smiling at each other, ahhhing and oooing a bit, and feeling *very* positive about the house; then we descended the stairs. The basement was lit like Yankee Stadium for a night game and sparkling clean. Nothing, *nothing* was stored there and every inch had been newly painted with a high-gloss gray enamel so that the floor shone like the deck of a new boat. As I walked about a sensation of foreboding welled up in me—something was definitely wrong. Sure enough, in the far corner behind a partition was the sump pump. It had not been running and did not run while we were in the house, but later I was sorry that I hadn't looked to see if it had been unplugged in honor of our visit. Outdoors (this was in February) we saw a huge, thick sheet of ice near the corner of the house where the pump was located. That pump was obviously throwing the water out of the basement into the backyard where it had frozen into a glacial flow. Needless to say, we were no longer interested.

Cracks in the foundation are another feature which often frightens buyers. Small cracks are not usually a serious problem. It is a rare foundation that never has a single crack. Deep long cracks, however, can be an indication of uneven settling and should be eyed with suspicion. Grossly uneven settling can undermine the structural soundness of a house. Be especially mindful of settling in areas of very uneven terrain or in areas where a great deal of fill was used on the lot.

There are a few simple checks for settling in a house. While you are inspecting the living areas of the house, place a marble or a small ball in the center of an uncarpeted floor and watch to see if it rolls, in which direction it rolls, and how fast. A slight tilt to the floor is not a major problem, but if the ball rolls the same way in every room and rolls quickly, you may have a house that has settled to one side. Also look at the corners of the doors and windows; diagonal cracks in the plaster or wallboard from the corner of the doorjamb toward the ceiling usually indicate uneven settling. Here again an occasional small crack is not a danger signal, since all houses settle; but keep an eye out for long cracks at various locations. Too many and too long spell trouble.

Back in the basement: Most people believe that soft wood in the beams of a house indicates termites. This is not necessarily the case. Termites start at the outside of a house and work inward. By the time the wood is soft in the central part of the basement, most of the house would be infested (and eaten). If you take a pocketknife or ice pick and find some soft spots in the wood near the center of the house, it is likely to be dry rot. A small isolated spot or two of dry rot should not mean disqualification for a house, but if there are several or if the knife goes in easily several inches, you may have uncovered a serious problem.

Soft spots in the wood near the outer wall of the foundation are more likely to indicate the location of termite damage. Since termites come into the house from outdoors, literally eating their way in, they are most likely to do the most damage and therefore to be discovered along the perimeter of the basement.

Termites are even easier to detect from the outside of the house. They cannot stand exposure to sunlight. Because of this, they enter a house by building mud tunnels up the walls of the foundation. These tunnels look like half circles about the diameter of a pencil and extend from the ground upward under the shingles. Inspect with extra care in the warmer parts of this country and in houses built upon loose soil or near a woods, for termites like these conditions best.

If you find termite mud tunnels on a house which you are seriously considering, don't push the panic button. Whereas a buyer's fear of water in the basement is a justifiable one, the fear of termites is far out of proportion to the damage that is usually done and to the cost of repair. Except in rare cases, termites are a problem which can be solved. They can be eliminated by a reputable company at a cost usually numbering in the hundreds of dollars, and a guarantee against reinfestation usually accompanies the service.

Although termites should not usually prevent you from buying a house, do *not* sign any contract to buy without a termite inspection clause. This clause provides for inspection by a reputable company and usually states that the sellers will repair the damage and have the termites eliminated if infestation is present. The clause stipulates that elimination and repairs will be at the seller's expense and will be completed prior to closing. If the sellers refuse to comply with this clause, the buyers have the option of voiding the contract with the full refund of their deposit money. The cost of inspection is usually paid by the buyers, but it is a nominal amount, usually carries a year's guarantee, and is worth every penny in peace of mind.

Back in the basement (again). This is also the best place to evaluate the plumbing. Older houses (thirty years plus) are likely to have at least some cast-iron pipe. These pipes are less desirable than copper since they are susceptible to rust and accumulated mineral deposits which diminish the usable interior diameter of the pipe, thus diminishing the accessibility of the water to the house. You can test for copper pipes by taking a small magnet along on your house hunt trips. If the pipes are copper, the magnet will not respond; if they are cast iron, the magnet will be attracted.

While your thoughts are on plumbing, take a look at the water heater. Is it an adequate size for your family? A forty-gallon tank might accommodate a small family, but when and if several additions come along, an eighty-gallon hot water heater may well top your Christmas list.

Another question to ask the seller: How old is the water heater? Most modern tanks last from eight to twelve years, some longer. We didn't know this fact in our first house, which was fourteen years old when we bought it and still had the original water heater. One morning when carrying a basket full of laundry to the washing machine in the basement, I stepped from the bottom stair into a flood. The water heater had sprung a leak during the night and as the water ran out of the bottom of the tank it automatically continued to fill. It took us two days to clean up the mess.

In houses which have circulating hot water heat, many builders install hot water systems which work off the furnace. Two of our houses have had hot water heated by the furnace in this manner and our experiences with it have not been positive. The storage tanks for these systems are almost always too small. I love long, deep, luxurious, *hot* baths, and there was never enough hot water for even one tubful. (I grumbled so much that occasionally my husband would heat the water on the stove and carry it to the tub—truly a love gift!) I think though that his problem with the hot water was even worse than mine, for he is a shower person. I can't even count the

number of times he would be happily soaping in the shower
only to be deluged by icy cold water.

Inadequacy of supply is unfortunately not the only problem
with these systems. With off-the-furnace water heating you
must keep that furnace running all summer in order to have
hot water. So consider a separate gas or electric hot water
heater as a definite plus in your house evaluations.

While in the basement most people walk over and look at
the furnace; and most of them see nothing. It is impossible to
judge quality, efficiency, and capacity by looking at a metal
shell or an old-fashioned steam boiler. You should ask how old
it is. A good furnace will usually last about twenty years. You
might also look about for evidence of singeing or soot; too
much soot may indicate faulty firing.

Aside from the clues around the furnace, the best way
to test the heating system is to turn on the heat. This is best
done when the owners are not in the house, but if they are at
home and it's winter, ask permission to turn up the heat.
Turn it up high. Glance at your watch to check the time, and
then continue with your inspection. When you begin to feel
the change in temperature, check your watch again. A forced
hot air system should change the temperature within ten minutes; a circulating hot water system may take twenty to thirty
minutes. When you begin to feel warm, go to the room that is
farthest from the furnace. Does it feel warm also? Simple as
this procedure sounds, it is really your most effective way of
evaluating the capacity and efficiency of the heating system,
for the essential goal of the system is, after all, warmth and
comfort. Also effective, however, is listening to the system. It
should run smoothly and unobtrusively, without excess bang-
ing and groaning.

If the heating system in the house you are considering is a
hot water system, it may be a zone type. Zone heating allows
you to keep the unused portions of the house at a cooler temperature. These systems usually result in a savings in dollars

and an increase in comfort. If the heating system is forced hot air, be sure to check to see if there is a humidification system on the furnace. Without a furnace humidifier, the air in the house becomes extremely dry in winter, a condition which is bad for furniture and human noses. One advantage of forced hot air heat, however, is the ease with which central air conditioning can be installed. These costs are greatly reduced because air conditioning equipment can make use of existing ducts. Electric heat has been installed in some newer homes, although it is not yet widely popular. It has the advantages of individual room thermostats, quiet operation, and cleanliness, but it is usually quite expensive.

Checking the heating system may be somewhat difficult in the heat of July, and you might feel a bit foolish turning on the furnace. But do try to do this. It might save you from great discomfort and a major expense in the cold of January.

When you are seriously considering a house, ask the owner what the *actual* cost of heating the house was for the previous winter. These costs are available from the gas, oil, or electric company which services the house. Weigh this cost in relation to how many people live in the house. Is it the home of two working adults where the heat is turned down all day with a minimal opening of doors or, at the other extreme, is it a home with several small children?

The age of the house you are considering might well affect its heating costs. Most houses built before World War II do not have full insulation and much heat will therefore escape. If you are house hunting in winter, you can test for insulation simply by placing your hand first on an outside wall and then on an inside wall. How much difference is there in the "feel" of the two walls? Almost all houses built after 1955 do have wall insulation. How effective it is, however, often depends on the overall construction of the house and on siting. A house with much wall space having a northern exposure will be colder, so make a mental note of which and how many rooms face north.

While you are observing a house's siting, also take note of how much shelter it has from the wind. The house where we now live is located near the top of a small mountain. It is a warm house, however, because it is surrounded by trees and because the land continues to rise for two more streets above us, thus sheltering us from the wind. Friends of ours live less than a half mile away, actually on top of "our" mountain. Their heating costs are almost one and a half times ours. Why? They are constantly buffeted by the wind in winter. They tell me that they can actually hear the groaning and shaking of the whole house in a storm. They do have a magnificent view, but they pay for it in heating costs.

Thorough inspection of the main living areas of a house is difficult to do properly if the owners are at home. No matter how necessary it is, how you describe it, or how delicately you do it, poking into the private corners of another person's home is intrusive, and the intrusion is least felt when unseen. If you are seriously interested in a house, therefore, return to see it a second time when your Realtor has made arrangements for the owners to be away. Then inspect thoroughly, and don't be self-conscious about your thoroughness. *It's your money.*

If on your first tour of a house only a small portion of the plumbing was visible to you in the basement, the reinspection trip is a good time to check it out further. Turn on as many faucets as you can, including the shower, and *then* flush the toilet. The water pressure may quite justifiably diminish, but it should *not* be reduced to a trickle. (This test is especially important in older houses where accumulated residue may be clogging cast-iron pipes.) Check the hot water. Is the pressure equal to the cold water? Test this on the faucet farthest from the hot water heater. How long does it take for the water from that faucet to get hot? *Does* it in fact get hot?

Next check the drainage. Nearly fill the tub, open the drain, and flush one or more toilets at the same time. The system should handle this without backup.

If the plumbing in the house seems satisfactory, your next

area of exploration should be the attic, even if this means that you have to crawl through a small opening in the top of a closet to get there. You can learn a great deal about the structure of the house by seeing its skeleton, and you can also learn a great deal about the condition of the roof by inspection of the rafters. Check first to be sure that the attic has adequate ventilation. Louvered vents are usually located in the vertical walls at either end of the attic, and sometimes additional vents are located under the eaves.

If you are satisfied that ventilation is adequate, check for water. Take a flashlight with a strong beam and move it along *each and every* rafter. Water runs down along wood and will stain it with a dark irregular pattern. Checking the rafters from the inside is an easy and dependable way to detect a leaky roof. Next beam the light along the floor. How much of the attic is actually floored? If all of it, try to see between the floorboards to check if there is insulation between the ceiling below and the attic floor. This insulation is extremely important since it prevents heat loss from the living areas of the house. And last but not least, while you are in the attic, check for signs of mice. You may see droppings scattered about or nests of torn or shredded material. A large nest or large droppings may also indicate a squirrel, which can do extensive damage.

If you climb out of the attic still interested in this particular house, you should continue poking about the main living area. Where carpets are not nailed down, check the floors underneath. Hardwood floors are preferable; however, many newer homes have wall-to-wall carpet laid over plywood subfloor. This is sometimes done even in the most expensive houses, and it is perfectly serviceable. When the carpet wears out, however, it must be replaced by new carpet. Area rugs and exposed floors are permanently ruled out.

Look also at the tile floors. Squares should not be separating with dirt accumulation in the cracks. Walk about on the tiles to test them. (Don't be afraid to move furniture; it is sometimes holding down the tile.) As you walk, listen for small snapping or cracking noises. These sounds indicate drying glue and loose tiles. Check inlaid floors for wear also. Some of the new highly padded styles cut very easily and you will see holes and scratches in them.

While you are looking at the floors, look also at the baseboards. There should not be gaps or large cracks where the baseboard moldings and floorboards meet. Open spaces and cracks here indicate settling and the use of green lumber in building.

Before you leave each room, stretch your neck muscles a bit and look up. Check each ceiling for signs of cracks, leakage stains, or weakening. In most newer houses, ceilings are made of the same "dry wall" material as walls. They should look smooth without visible signs of taping. In older houses, ceilings are plaster and deserve even more attention. When I was perhaps ten years old, the plaster ceiling in our living room caved in at 5:30 A.M. The tremendous crash startled everyone out of bed. Worse yet, it was expensive to repair and it took us months of cleaning to get the fine plaster dust out of *everything*.

During your reinspection trip, check the windows in several rooms. Do they slide up and down easily? Binding windows are another clue to uneven settling. Look also to see if the window frames are well maintained; because of high exposure to sunlight and changes in temperature, paint chips and peels first on the windowsills.

I hesitate at this point to go into an extensive discussion of painting and decoration because it is so much a matter of personal taste. For those with strong likes and dislikes, the decor should be irrelevant since they will probably redo the entire house to their liking anyway. For others, a clean, neat house in "move-in" condition can mean less work and therefore much satisfaction. The buyer undoubtedly pays for that move-in condition, however, as these houses invariably sell faster and at higher prices. If you are not a do-it-yourselfer and must hire professional painters and paperhangers, it is probably better to pay the extra for that "excellent condition" house. You finance this added cost in the mortgage, and unless you remain in the house until the mortgage is paid out, the *real* added cost to you rarely amounts to more than a few dollars a month. On the other hand, painters and paperhangers can be very expensive and must be paid out-of-pocket.

If you are a handyman-type family, however, don't pass a house up because it is dirty or badly decorated. You can often get *real* savings on this kind of house. I never cease to be surprised at how much decorating and tidiness affect prospective buyers. I have seen people turn away from perfectly good houses because of color scheme and/or clutter.

I originally showed the house where we now live to customers. When we walked in, we were greeted by rooms filled with too much furniture obviously collected over many years and from many places. The walls looked as though they had been painted and papered by color-blind opportunists. My customers were aggravated with me. They felt that I was wasting their time showing them this "awful" house. They could not see the secluded location, the spacious five bedrooms, the excellent traffic pattern. Their interest stopped when they saw the wallpaper.

When you make your appointment for reinspection, be sure you will have plenty of daylight time for inspecting the exterior as well as the interior of the house. Painting a house can cost several hundred dollars and take a lot of time. The need for painting in itself should not be a deterrent to buying, but it should certainly be a negotiating point in the price. One word of caution: if the paint seems to be blistering in several places, pierce one of these blisters, take off the flaking paint, and feel the wood under it. If there is moisture present or you can feel a certain dampness, it can be indicative of a potential recurring problem. If moisture from green lumber or from rain during construction is trapped in the shingles, you will be forever repainting that house. One family we know had to completely reshingle their house because of trapped moisture.

While walking around the house, check the gutters and downspouts. These are areas of high moisture and quick rotting of wood. Aluminum gutters and downspouts are of course preferable since they do not rust and are therefore serviceable for a longer period of time.

If at all possible, go up on top of the roof. Look for loose, curling shingles or particularly brittle ones. Check also for signs of patching. An asphalt shingle roof should last for about fifteen years in cool climates, somewhat less in the warmer areas of the country.

If you are fortunate enough to find a brick house, your maintenance time and expense will be restricted to trim areas. Stucco also requires minimum maintenance in the South or in areas where there are no wide fluctuations of temperature, but be extremely careful of stucco houses in all of the northern areas of this country. Stucco has no joints and therefore is adversely affected by the contracting and expanding caused by changes in temperature. Aluminum and vinyl siding are now popular also since they are durable and essentially maintenance free.

Before you begin your inspection of the exterior of the house, you should know if it uses sewers or a septic tank for waste disposal. A good working septic system is not a detriment; however, a faulty tank or improper and/or inefficient drainage can be an ever-present problem and a difficult one to live with. On a hot summer day, especially after a rain, all the equipment you may need to find the answer to the septic tank question is your nose. But if the smell test is not applicable, have the agent ask the owner for the location of the tank and the leach lines and/or dry well. Then, as I mentioned when we discussed location, walk the property. Spongy circles which have a distinctive odor and perhaps numerous minuscule insects are a dead giveaway. Standing pools of water about the property also indicate poor drainage, which usually adversely affects waste disposal. Septic tank and drainage problems are not only expensive to correct but also something of a health hazard if there is surface seepage of the waste. It is difficult to live in a house where you cannot always flush the toilet or do the wash for fear of septic tank backup, which in itself is a *very* unpleasant experience.

After reading this list of potential problems you may be tempted to say "What's wrong with it?" every time you enter a house. In this respect, however, selling real estate is very *unlike* selling used cars. (Real estate agents are always being compared to used-car salesmen.) Generally, people *do not* sell a house because it has a problem. The legal costs involved in selling, the commissions, and most of all the disruption of the family's personal life combine to motivate most people to have a problem repaired or to "live with it" rather than to sell the house. In the case of the repaired problem, its discovery and repair are a definite plus; but do check the quality of the repair work if you can. In the case of the live-with-it problem, you must try to spot it in your inspection, and then you must decide whether or not you too want to live with it or take on the cost of repair.

In many urban and suburban areas, especially where large corporate offices are located, there is an alternative to self-inspection. The business of professional house inspection is growing rapidly. These companies train inspectors to evaluate the structure and condition of the house and its working systems. Most of them work with a rather thick inspection manual, a long checklist, ladders, lights, and a rather large block of time. After the inspection, they provide the buyer with a written report, usually several pages in length, evaluating all aspects of the property. Many companies also include a guarantee of a year to eighteen months in their fee. These fees vary considerably from one company to another and from one area of the country to another. The best procedure, therefore, if you choose to use an inspection service, is to call several and compare price and service. You might also ask your sales agent if he has worked with any of these companies and would be able to give you an evaluation of their efficiency.

There is one distinct advantage in using an inspection company in that the sale itself can be made contingent upon a favorable report. This can be written into the contract so that a report indicating serious flaws in the house will allow the buyer the option of cancelling the contract *without* loss of deposit monies.

If home inspection agencies are not available in the area of your house hunting or if you choose not to use one, you can and should do the inspection yourself, noting on paper any misgivings you may have, however slight. If these misgivings cannot be resolved to your satisfaction (if you have trouble sleeping that night) have your lawyer add a clause to the contract that the purchase is dependent upon an inspection by a competent plumber, heating contractor, roofer, or whatever the problem requires, and a report of satisfactory condition. This report will ease the pre-closing jitters and may save you from the fate of our fairy-tale couple in their castle on the glass mountain.

# Working with a Sales Agent

Quotes from my work week:
"What a great job for a woman with children."
"It must be interesting for you, seeing all those houses."
"What a pleasant way to spend an afternoon."

At one point or another, most women buyers and many men think that they would like to sell real estate. My job is imagined as a kind of "Gardens in May" house tour which I spend browsing, admiring, and gently conducting "guests" from house to house.

Would that it were! But let me tell you about it, for I think understanding something of the job will help you first to evaluate what a good agent can and should do for you and then to approach the role of customer more effectively (and successfully).

Perhaps the most important thing to remember is that no matter what we call ourselves—Realtors, Realtor-Associates, brokers, agents, etc.—a real estate agent is a *salesman*. As a salesman, his prime function is *to sell*.

(I use the word sales*man* here and the masculine pronouns simply as a matter of convenience. I mean always to refer to *both* men and women agents. In fact, in many areas of this country, women sales agents outnumber men sales agents.)

The nature of the real estate business makes the job of selling more complex, demanding, and difficult than most other sales jobs. The product (houses) cannot be gathered together and displayed in a showroom; a customer cannot take a "test

94

drive"; and a sample cannot be presented from a sample case and then ordered for immediate delivery. None of these procedures works because each house is unique and in a unique location. Furthermore, sale and purchase in the real estate business always involves legal commitments, usually borrowed money, and often a good deal of emotional strain.

In addition to the problems inherent in the product, there is the complexity of the working procedure. The showing of houses is to the real estate agent what the time spent on stage is to the actor. It is his hour in the spotlight. Its effectiveness, however, is dependent on many hours of "offstage" work and a great deal of personal knowledge, skill, and talent. The offstage work saves the customer time; the knowledge, skill, and talent protect the future growth of the customer's investment.

Let's look at the "work" part first. What do I do when not showing houses to customers? Part of my time is spent keeping up with an ever-changing "product." This means knowing the market. "Knowing the market" means checking and filing by town each day's new listings (there are often as many as fifteen a day on the large MLS board where I work), noting changes in prices and terms, marking houses which are "on deposit" or sold, going to open houses, preinspecting houses which might be of interest to my customers, and driving about to locate properties which are not familiar to me.

When an agent knows the market, when he is totally familiar with the properties available for sale, he need only get to know his customers in order to begin the task of matching house and buyer. This saves a great deal of "fumbling about" time. It is a mark of sloppy workmanship in the real estate trade when you see an agent whip out his map of the area and say, "Let's see. It seems to me that the house is around here somewhere." A good agent knows his territory, knows the buyer's needs, and has found and inspected the houses *before* going out with customers. And of course, if every agent were a "good agent," house hunting would take less time and be less exhausting.

Being a good agent means more than legwork, however. This is where the knowledge, skill, and talent come in. The agent should *know*, should actively and continually gather information about, the communities which he serves. He should have the answers to questions on taxes, schools, plans of the local zoning boards, proposed road and industrial construction, and proposed residential construction. The agent must also be entirely familiar with the mortgage market, including qualification requirements and interest rates at all the banks and lending institutions in the area. If your salesman cannot answer your questions, you should not be working with him, for this is information which is vital to *your* success.

An agent's skill and talent come into play when decisions based on judgment are called for. This includes selecting houses which appeal to the particular buying family, informing the buyers about the "character" of each of the area towns, and most important of all, negotiating.

Negotiating is never taught in real estate school. Some agents are "naturals," some learn rapidly and are extremely effective early in their careers, some are little more than messengers. Since the buyer cannot watch his agent negotiating, evaluation of his performance is somewhat difficult. More often than not it comes down to "Were you successful in getting my price?" Usually an agent who has survived in the business for three years or more, who is well informed, and who answers your questions honestly and tactfully will turn out to be good at negotiation. It's really a matter of survival of the fittest.

After negotiation is complete and the price agreed upon, there is still work to be done. Much of my time is spent on the "paper work": reporting the sale to the MLS (multiple listing service); running contracts between buyers, sellers, and lawyers; depositing and transferring escrow monies; and filling out mortgage applications with buyers.

At this point the real estate agent finds himself playing two very different roles, errand boy and financial counselor. It is not unusual for him to return to open a house three or four times after the contracts are signed to allow appraisers or inspectors in, to have utilities turned on or off, and often to let the buyers measure windows or match paint and fabric swatches. Despite all this running, the agent does not receive his commission until the closing, by which time it is usually well earned.

All of the activity which I've just described is centered pretty much around the "product" of this business, houses. There is, however, yet another dimension to this complex job. The added dimension is people—the individual personalities, needs, and demands of the buyers and sellers (and sometimes the lawyers). It is, of course, the people which make each situation, each sale, unique and challenging.

Working with buyers begins with getting to know them. Unless the customer insists on going out immediately or "meeting at the house," the well-trained agent will spend some time in the office in order to save a great deal of time on the road. You will find him asking personal questions. He needs to know your yearly gross income, the amount of your savings, the amount of money you will use as a down payment, and the amount and terms of any large outstanding debts which you might have. This gathering of financial information is akin to taking a patient's history in the field of medicine, and it is just as essential to the diagnosis and treatment of "homeitis." In the real estate business this procedure is called qualification and it will be repeated again (almost exactly) when you apply for a mortgage, so keep the figures handy.

Many new agents are shy about qualifying people because of the personal questions which must be asked. As a result the buyers waste much time looking at inappropriate properties. Since house price, taxes, interest rate, mortgage term, and family income are inextricably interrelated, it is impossible for the agent to choose properties for inspection without adequate financial information.

Informal "getting acquainted" time in the office is almost as important as qualification. Facts and figures aside, an agent must know his *people* in order to serve them. It is a good idea to talk about yourselves when you and your family meet the agent. Tell him about your life-style, hobbies, interests, etc. Bring along a "need and want" list if you can, and rate the wants in order of priority.

Another aspect of the sales agent's job is somewhat related to that of a social secretary or perhaps a travel agent. Each House Hunt outing must be planned for maximum exposure with minimum fatigue. Most people do not allow enough time. Touring from house to house is a difficult and tiring activity and should be practiced with several days' rest between each excursion.

The only exception to this rule is the corporate transfer family. In the transfer situation the buyers usually have a week or so to find a suitable house. They must see as much of the market as possible in order to make their choice from among the available properties. Therefore they must house-hunt every day, trying at first to get an overview of a different town or area each day, and later in the week returning to those areas or houses which they found most appealing.

Even under the pressure of transfer, however, a competent agent will take care that no one day is too long. It has been my experience that five, or at the most six, houses is full capacity for a day's hunting, especially if combined with an introductory tour of the area. After six houses, buyers lose all perspective on what they have seen. Property, structure, floor plans, features blur together and "discussions" arise over which house had what. An agent's planning, market research, and familiarity with his customers should make longer trips unnecessary. He should select houses within a limited geographical area and the route should be traced on a large wall map before leaving the office. In this way the buyers know where they've been and where they're going. In the course of the tour, an agent working familiar ground will point out schools, churches, shopping centers, medical and recreational facilities, and business and industrial areas. He will *not* need a map to do so.

You know now what you can expect of the good agent. Like most relationships, however, that of customer/agent is a give and take. The actions of the customer can also affect the success of the house hunt, and patterns of customer behavior range from bad to good to better to best. It would be an insult to your intelligence to dwell upon the obvious First Commandment for all "good" real estate customers: "Be honest and open regarding your financial status and housing needs." So let me move on to some more subtle points.

When your good agent has brought you to a house which you "love," try to resist the temptation to return the same day. Go home, calm down, eat dinner, and sleep on it. Then request to return for reinspection the following day or the following weekend. You will look at the property with new eyes unjaded by fatigue. If on your return you feel yourselves "falling even more deeply in love with the place," you may do a thorough inspection then, or even better, make a third appointment for a buying inspection.

*Under no circumstances should you buy a house the first time you see it.* You must simply take this advice on trust, for there is no "authority" to back me up. I have learned, however, that people do not *see* a house the first time through, they feel it. I have often asked buyers specific questions about the houses they have looked at and expressed interest in, and I have been amazed at the inaccuracy of their perceptions. Usually they focus on a few features, often visualizing these features with some degree of exaggeration. They have either no memory or a rather inaccurate memory of the remainder of the house. So I repeat, return several times, and don't feel embarrassed or apologetic if you change your mind after the third time back. It happens all the time and agents are accustomed to it.

When you return the second time, take a pad and pencil and a long tape measure with you. (If your agent is well trained, he will carry a fifty-foot tape in his car.) Sketch a floor plan with dimensions and indications of door and window locations. Before you return home, ask for a copy of the real estate listing.

When you think you are ready to buy, wait one more day. It is most important that you do not make an offer while riding the crest of a buying wave which is about to crash on a very real and rocky shore. Under no circumstances should you "give it a try" at a low price before you are sure you have the right house. An offer is serious business and if made too soon (before you are certain of your decision), panic usually follows along with a 7 A.M. phone call to the agent to say that the offer is withdrawn. This act is usually followed by so much embarrassment on the part of the buyers that they find another agent even though they might have been well pleased with the service they were getting.

When working with an agent, remember also that you should work with him completely, allowing him to do all aspects of his job. The aspect most often ignored is that of middleman, or go-between, yet it is one of his most crucial functions. Whether you have a question about the cost of heating or the quality of the water, let the agent ask it. The buying and selling of houses has so many emotional aspects that it is always better to have an intermediary who can keep things on a rational plane. I have seen many instances of personality clashes between buyers and sellers which resulted in stalemates of feudlike intensity.

I have also seen instances of a perfectly innocent comment breaking up a sale. One couple I worked with was pleased that a house which they liked was located near the school which their children would attend. The sellers returned as we were leaving from a very positive reinspection trip. There was nothing I could do in courtesy except introduce them.

"We love your house," said Mrs. Buyer.

"Yes, and it's in such good condition," said Mr. Buyer.

"Oh, you'll find everything is perfect here," said Mrs.

Seller, "and you'll get used to the school kids going by after a while."

An innocent comment. But it planted a seed of doubt. I don't believe the buyers would have been disturbed by the passage of the children by their house twice a day. They had children of their own and the house was *not* located in a cut-across pathway. The sellers were older people and resented the intrusion of schoolchildren's noises. But the comment did its damage, for the buyers became worried about resale and decided against the house. The sellers lost a sale. The buyers lost more. They lost a house which would have been both good for them and a good investment since those "schoolchildren's noises" are not nearly as objectionable as the noise of a heavily traveled road or a nearby industrial complex, and few buyers would find them intrusive.

Money talk is of course the ultimate question between buyer and seller, and it should be done only through the agent. Closing dates and unusual contract specifications are part of money talk and should be presented at the same time as price. But we are getting into negotiation, and I want to save that for the next chapter. Just remember here that the emotional tension of bargaining for a "home" needs the practiced, cool hand of the mediator.

By law in most states, all offers on a house which is under a listing contract must be made through the agent with whom you first saw the house. This holds true even if you saw the house three weeks ago with Agent 1, and you are now working most happily with Agent 2. The trouble usually develops thus: Agent 2 drives you up to the house. You say, "I think we saw this one already."

"Well, take another look," he says—a move decidedly against all real estate training but all too often practiced. Going through again, you decide you like it. Your offer should be through Agent 1, even though Agent 2 showed you the house the second time. If you make the offer through Agent 2 and Agent 1 gets word of it, you might tie the whole deal up in a legal dispute over commissions. There have been some nasty court battles over this type of situation, but the decision almost always favors Agent 1 as the original agent to bring buyer in contact with the property. This holds true, however, *only* if Agent 1 actually walked on the property with you. If you only drove by with him, there is no obligation.

Given now that you have found a house which you are sure you want to buy and which you can afford. You make your offer through the agent with whom you saw the property, and he presents it to the sellers. The agent is under legal obligation to report all the facts and figures mentioned during negotiation accurately and completely to both parties. This is so serious a trust that in most states failure to report all material or misrepresentation of material can result in the loss of the agent's license.

Thus the accuracy of the letters and numbers of negotiation is controlled. The manner of negotiation, however, is not controlled. It is a tremendously variable manifestation of the agent's personality and skill, and it greatly affects the sale. This is the pressure point of the real estate business. The ability to hold up through negotiation separates successful agents from dropouts. As I said earlier, those who survive for three years or more are usually good at negotiation and therefore usually successful agents.

Being a successful agent, however, is not necessarily synonymous with being a good agent, since there's more to service than negotiation. You, of course, want to work with a good *and* successful agent. So how do you find one?

It's a little like finding a good dentist or a good piano teacher. The brand-new ones may be enthusiastic but they usually have much to learn from experience, and the effectiveness of the "old pros" cannot always be evaluated by credentials or time on the job. So as with the dentist or the piano teacher, the classic method is the referral.

If you have friends or acquaintances who have recently

bought a house, ask them about the agents that they worked with. Look for more than an evaluation of personality, however. "He's a great guy" doesn't say anything about technical competence. Ask your friends: "What did the agent do for you? Did he know the area? How were negotiations handled? Where did you think he was strong? Where weak?"

Even better than referrals are the experiences which you may have had while warming up. Check back through the cards you collected while just looking and the evaluations you made then. Good rapport between agent and customer is essential and very definitely a matter of individual taste. The right agent for your friends may not be right for you.

If you did not have time for a warm-up, if you are a transferee, or if you know of no one who has recently bought a house, you must use the hit-or-miss method. This involves choosing an agency from the Yellow Pages or calling about an ad in the newspaper and making an appointment to see the house being advertised. While you are with the agent *the first time*, evaluate his ability by asking questions and by making observations on his competence based on the working procedure which I discussed at the beginning of this chapter.

If you are considering a wide geographical area for your house hunt, you should plan to work with several agents. Real estate is a local activity best served by local people. An agent's familiarity with an area can save you thousands of dollars and assure you of a good investment. Therefore tell your agent freely and without embarrassment that you are working with him locally. Specifically name the towns which you want him to cover and tell him that you will be working with another agent in the more distant areas.

Some agencies will refer you to their branch offices in other towns; others may be able to supply you with the names of agents with whom they have previously worked. If this kind of referral is made, you should take the time to meet the person to whom you are referred, but remember that you are not under any obligation to work with him.

This brings me to the question of affiliations. In many parts of the country, large franchise real estate companies are springing up. Century 21, Red Carpet Realtors, and Better Homes and Gardens are examples. You should understand how these business operations work. They are not one corporation, one agency, or even one "big, happy family." Despite gimmicks like flags, company colors, and uniforms for salesmen, they are very loosely tied groups of individual agencies. Independent brokers "join" the parent firm to advertise together and to assume the "image" which the parent firm has established after considerable cash outlay on Madison Avenue or its local equivalent. The theory is that if buyers and sellers (i.e., people) can be sold on the idea that Happy House Nationwide is *the* place to buy real estate, they will call a Happy House Nationwide office whenever and wherever they want to buy and/or sell. These franchise organizations have some standards as to size, operating procedures, and referrals, but each independently owned office very definitely has its own personality. In general I see neither advantage nor disadvantage to working with these firms. Judge them individually, as you would any other firm.

Akin to the national franchise is the national referral service. Some large corporations which transfer executives frequently and many independent brokers belong to these services. Home to Home, Relo, All Points, and Homes for Living are a few of the many names which you may have heard. The services of relocation agencies vary greatly in both scope and efficiency. Some do provide the transferred family with a great deal of information and take great care to refer them to a reputable agency. Others are nothing more than a phone book of member agencies which have agreed to pay a referral fee to any other member firm which sends them a customer.

I am, of course, not familiar with all the relocation services across the country and would hardly think to try to evaluate them individually. In general, however, I feel that the major benefit goes to the agencies, which share referral fees. On the

other hand, there is little or no harm to the buyers. It is something of a gimmick, but a rather harmless one since you as
buyer have no obligation to remain with any sales agent. If
nothing more, the referral service provides you with a place to
begin in a new town.

In some parts of the country, especially around major cities,
you will see the big blue and white "R" Realtor symbol in
every office you enter. The "independent" unaffiliated broker
is not to be found. Being a Realtor denotes membership in an
association, but an association different from the franchise or
the relocation service. Franchise members and relocation
service members are almost always Realtors also. The word
*Realtor* and the "R" symbol are registered trademarks which
represent members of the National Association of Realtors and
the member local and state boards. These firms subscribe to a
given code of ethics, usually on display in each office, and
they agree to share their listings on a central board.

Let me explain how this works. When a person lists his
house for sale, he enters into a contract with the real estate
broker to act as his agent. This is usually an "exclusive-right-
to-sell" contract, which means that the broker alone has the
right to sell the house. (Even if the owner sells it himself after
the listing contract has been signed, he must still pay the
agent's commission.) At one time these so-called exclusives
made house hunting a very time-consuming process, since a
buyer had to visit each office to see its exclusive listings. Now
Realtors have joined into local real estate boards where they
display their exclusive listings by means of published sheets,
books, or cards. They submit the listings to the board in order
to share the right to sell the properties with all the other members of that board. This listing pool is called the Multiple
Listing Service. When an MLS property is sold, the commission is split by mutual agreement between the selling office
and the listing office.

Occasionally some sellers do not want their houses listed on
MLS. These houses are shown only by the agency with which

the seller signed the listing contract. Information about the property is not distributed to other members of the Realtor Board.

In more rural areas of this country, you will still find many brokers who are not Realtors and who do not belong to Realtor Boards. In these areas you must visit each independent real estate office in order to see that agency's listings. This time-consuming chore can be somewhat abbreviated by watching the classified section of the local newspaper for several weeks in a row. You will see advertising patterns develop, and you will soon recognize one house from another. If you particularly like working with one independent broker, tell him about the house which another independent is advertising. He will call that broker and ask for cooperation on the listing. Most brokers will "co-broke" in this way, thus allowing you to continue to work with an agent whom you think competent. If the listing broker refuses to cooperate with your sales agent, you must see the house through the agency which is advertising it, but you need not look at any other houses with them and you can immediately return to working with your former agent if you do not choose to buy that particular house.

Whether you are house hunting in the suburbs or in the country, whether you are working with a Realtor or an independent broker, there are some general tips for greater efficiency which you should know. Most important of these is: Go in the agent's car. This gives him an opportunity to point out features of the town and of the neighborhoods which you pass, and it gives you the opportunity to ask questions. Those pseudosophisticates who feel worldly because they disdain to be driven around by a salesman, preferring to follow in their own car, are merely wasting gas. Caravans are inconvenient, inefficient, and expensive.

For reinspections, however, it really is preferable to meet the agent at the house with your own car. This gives you, the buyers, the opportunity to talk privately en route both to and from the house and/or to the agent's office. There the two of you can confer with him or question him as a unit, having discussed personal issues privately.

If at all possible, do not take the children house-hunting. They quickly become bored and they tend to be distracting. Very young children are often a problem since they like to touch both things and animals. This can be agonizing to sellers, buyers (parents), and nervous sales agents, to say nothing of its being potentially dangerous to a child. When you are seriously considering a house and are returning a second time, then take the children. Let them see the house and express their opinions. They will feel that they are part of the decision and the trauma of moving will be slightly alleviated by the anticipation of the new house.

Do take a notebook along on every house-hunt trip. Take notes on houses that especially appeal to you and on statements of value which the agent may make in passing.

When a piece of property interests you, ask the agent to make a copy of the listing for you. Practically every real estate office now has some kind of quick copy machine, and a photocopy of the listing can save long hours of "do you remember which house had. . . ."

If you decide to look at "for sale by owner" houses (and you definitely should), you should be aware of several factors. It has been my experience that most homeowners' sales are overpriced. The sellers are selling their home, not a house, and they hope to be paid for their emotional attachment to that home. Therefore if you should like what you see in a private-sale house, be sure you do some good comparison shopping before making an offer. You should also be prepared to inspect carefully. This may prove to be somewhat embarrassing and difficult since the sellers will most likely want to be in the house while you do the inspection. Do it anyway. It's your money.

If you make an offer on a private-sale house and come to an agreement on price and terms, shake hands. *Do not leave a deposit check.* This situation differs from the listed house where you must give the agent an earnest-money check in order to make the offer. The check given to an agent is held in the broker's trust account and will be returned to you if the offer is refused or the contracts are not signed. There is no such trust account in the private sale, and you may have great difficulty getting your money returned if you change your mind in the morning or if the lawyers can't work out a mutually agreeable contract. Once the contract is drawn and signed in the private sale, one of the lawyers will act as fiduciary (trust) agent and hold all deposit monies.

Before I leave the topic of sales agents, I'd like to say a word about guilt feelings. This may sound unbelievable, but I have seen people make offers to please an agent. Feeling obligated for his time and knowing he is paid only by commission, they want to buy *something* and proceed to make an offer on a house which they are willing to "settle for." Insane, but it happens. I have also seen people stop reading homeowners' ads because they feel loyal to their hard-working agent.

Do not fall into this trap. To repeat: A real estate agent is a salesman. Showing houses is his job. Every day brings cancellations and disappointments, and almost every week brings the news that someone with whom he has been working has bought a house through another agent. It happens. It's part of the job.

I worked for almost a year with very close friends of ours, showing them a great many houses and spending much time with them. One day I answered my home phone to hear, "Carolyn, what Broadway play would you like to see?" My friends had bought a house privately from a mutual acquaintance. They felt guilty and obliged to me for my time and efforts. What did I feel? Disappointment, yes. Resentment? Anger? No. (And we are still close friends.) The experience was a reaffirmation of the paramount rule of House Hunt: Each person must act first and always in his own best interest.

# Negotiating

Now we approach the climax. Everything you've read so far leads to this chapter. Yet this very chapter is omitted from most books on real estate.

Why? It's difficult to write. Difficult because the subject matter is difficult to organize and difficult to explain. Negotiating is an art. You might say that it's the creative part of every real estate transaction. Its success depends not only on trainable, teachable skills and "procedures," but equally upon the interplay of personalities, the subtlety of interpretation, response, and reaction, and the uncertainty of projection. How does one "explain" a thing like that?

Negotiating is also the most nerve-racking and agonizing part of real estate. Involved people don't sleep at night. They can't eat, or they eat constantly. Ashtrays fill, paths get worn in carpets, and children whisper to each other that Mom and Dad are crabby today.

The real estate marketplace is one of the few areas of financial exchange in this country where even the most refined and sophisticated members of our society openly condone haggling. It is fashionable to be difficult in bargaining, to yield slowly point for point on price and terms. It is also an excellent release for pent-up aggressions.

Couch it in contracts, courtesies, forms, procedures, whatever, each real estate deal is a replay of the scene between the turn-of-the-century pushcart peddler and his customer. The questions are timeless and classless: "How much do you want?" "How much will you give?" The drama, the acts, the games people play are also ageless.

*Bargaining scene I:*
    CUSTOMER: "You gotta be kidding. I can do better any place in town."
    He turns and begins to walk away.
    NAME OF THE GAME: Call Me Back.
*Bargaining scene II:*
    PEDDLER: "You crazy. That's no deal."
    He turns his back and begins to dust his wares.
    NAME OF THE GAME: Bid Again.

Some people love this kind of game and are naturally good at it. For others, it is so excruciating that they cannot wait for the questions to be resolved, for the game to be over. Most of us fall somewhere in between. But love it or hate it, if you want to buy a house, you must face negotiating.

I can't promise you "success," for no amount of written words can possibly create a negotiating artist, and even the great artists in this field don't always succeed. What I can give you is insight, a kind of overview of what usually happens or can happen during the negotiation stage of House Hunt. In short, enough knowledge so that you'll have the blindfold off and be able to see what's happening.

Let's take a careful look at one fictitious "deal." Understanding that, we can then discuss some variations on the theme.

After six weeks in the real estate marketplace, Dick and Jane Hunter found exactly the four-bedroom colonial they had wanted.

Here's a replay of the action:

*In the real estate office, May 21.*
    DICK HUNTER: We'd like to make an offer of $83,000 on that colonial we liked on the hill.
    AGENT: That's great, but I know the owner won't take it. He

Price: $93,500.
Style: Colonial
Town: Happyville
Age: 12 years
No. of rooms: 8
Taxes: $2,245.00
Lot size: ½ acre
Heat: Oil hot water
Garage: 2-car attached
Water: city
Sewer: septic
Basement: full, dry

First Floor: flagstone entry; LR (13 × 18); dining room (13 × 11); kitchen (13 × 19); family room (14 × 16) with fireplace, lavatory.

Second floor: master bedroom (13 × 16) with walk-in closet; three other bedrooms, two full baths.

*Note:* Dining room chandelier *not* included.

Owner: John & Martha Barter
      21 Winding Road
      Happyville, Connecticut    Phone 555-0003

To show: call for appointment or use keybox.

Listing Realtor: Happy House Nationwide    555-5432

Comm: 6%   3/3/79      7/3/79

---

refused $85,000 about six weeks ago. Can't you do a little better?

    DICK: $83,000 is our offer.

    AGENT: Okay. Let me get an offer form from the file. I'll also need a check from you for $500.

    *Dick makes out the check to Joe Welcome, Realtor, Trustee. They begin to fill out the offer form.*

AGENT: Closing date?

JANE: August 29.

AGENT: How much mortgage will you want on this house?

DICK: $55,000.

AGENT: Any extras to be included at that price?

JANE: Well, of course all the installed wall-to-wall carpet has to stay.

AGENT: Okay. I'll do the best I can for you, but don't get your hopes up because I really don't think they'll take it.

*Dick and Jane sign the offer form and leave the office.*

*The agent waits until just after dinner, when he thinks both owners of the house will be at home, and phones them.*

AGENT: Mr. Barter, this is Tom Sales from Joe Welcome, Realtors. I have an offer on your house.

MR. BARTER: Great. What's the offer.

AGENT: The figure is $83,000.

MR. BARTER: That's out of the question.

AGENT: Will you make a counteroffer, Mr. Barter?

MR. BARTER: Not at that price.

*The agent calls the Hunters.*

AGENT: Sorry, Dick, but Mr. Barter refused your offer.

DICK: Didn't he make a counteroffer?

AGENT: He said "Not at that price."

DICK: Huh, I see.

AGENT: Would you and Jane like to make another offer?

DICK: I don't know. We'll have to talk about it.

AGENT: Do that. I'll be in the office at nine tomorrow morning if you want to call me.

*May 22, 9:15 a.m. Phone rings in the office.*

AGENT: Good morning, Joe Welcome, Realtors. Tom Sales speaking.

DICK: Hi, Tom. This is Dick Hunter. We'd like to change our offer to $85,700.

AGENT: Okay, Dick. Any other changes?

DICK: No, everything else the same.

AGENT: Right, I'll let you know as soon as I can.

*Agent calls the Barters.*

AGENT: Mrs. Barter, this is Tom Sales from Joe Welcome, Realtors.

MRS. BARTER: Yes.

AGENT: My buyers have made another offer on your house.

MRS. BARTER: Oh really? Well, my husband is at his office closing things up right now, but you can get in touch with him there. The number is 555-5911.

AGENT: Thank you, Mrs. Barter. I'll call him right away.

*Agent phones.*

MR. BARTER: Barter speaking.

AGENT: Mr. Barter, this is Tom Sales. My buyers have made another offer on your house.

MR. BARTER: Yeah? At what price?

AGENT: They have raised their offer to $85,700. They're only looking for a mortgage of $55,000, and they're well-qualified buyers, Mr. Barter.

MR. BARTER: What's the close?

AGENT: August 29. They have sold their house and want to be in before school starts, so I'm sure that will be a firm date.

MR. BARTER: I'll have to talk with my wife. I'll call you tomorrow.

AGENT: Fine. If I'm not in the office when you call, just leave a message and I'll return your call as soon as I can.

*The agent calls Dick Hunter again and explains that they will have to wait until tomorrow for an answer.*

*May 23. Mr. Barter is speaking to Tom Sales on the phone.*

MR. BARTER: My wife and I discussed this for some time last night. We're willing to take $89,000 for the house, but not a penny less.

AGENT: Thank you, Mr. Barter. I'll tell the buyers and see if I can get them to come up again on their price.

MR. BARTER: Listen, don't be bothering me with anything less than $89,000. That's the lowest price we'll take.

*The agent calls Dick Hunter.*

AGENT: Dick, I talked with Mr. Barter. He *has* made a counteroffer, but I think it would be better if I got together with you and Jane tonight so that I can explain the situation to you.

DICK: Well, I'm curious, Tom. But okay. How about 8:30?

AGENT: Great, I'll come over to your place.

*8:30 at the Hunters'.*

AGENT: So he said that he would take 89, but not a penny less.

JANE: Gee, Tom, we really can't afford to go that high. We'd have to carry more mortgage and we'd have to put in every penny that we were saving for new furnishings and decorating.

DICK: Damn! Well, I guess we begin again. Anything new on the market in the last few days?

AGENT: Look, Dick, Jane. I don't think we should give up so easily. I know he said 89 was rock bottom, but give me a chance. Maybe I can talk him down a bit.

DICK: I don't know, Tom. We really shouldn't go any higher. We'll end up dry with no money for extras. I think we had better try to find someone who's more willing to compromise.

JANE: I agree with Dick. But I certainly did like that house.

AGENT: I have an idea. If we could get the Barters to include that dining room chandelier, the portable storage shed in the backyard, the fireplace equipment, the drapes and curtains throughout the house, and of course the rods and shades, all the carpeting, and the wrought-iron lawn furniture you were admiring, you could save enough money from out-of-pocket expenditures to make a higher offer.

DICK: Ummmmm. Yeah, that's true. That stuff must be worth a few thousand dollars anyway.

AGENT: And it would probably cost even more than that to buy it all new.

JANE: How about the freezer he has in the basement and the chain-link dog run he has in the back corner of the yard? We could really use those, too.

DICK: You think he'd throw all that in?

AGENT: Don't know. But it's worth a try. What could you offer if we got all that?

DICK: I don't know. What do you think, Jane?

JANE: Well, I guess we could go to $87,000. The drapes and the chandelier would probably come to that much.

DICK: Okay. Offer him 87.

AGENT: It's going to be tough. He was really firm on that eighty-nine. But let's give it a go. Oh, one thing though. What if we move the closing date up to July 29 instead of August 29? I think the guy is anxious to get going, and closing a month earlier might really help.

JANE: That's fine with me. It will give me a whole month to settle in before school starts and I have to go back to work.

DICK: Sounds okay to me, too. The people buying this house are in an apartment, so they're pretty flexible, but I know that they'd like to close as soon as it's convenient for us.

AGENT: Let's write it up then! (*He takes a new offer form out of his briefcase, fills it out, and tears up the old one.*) Now I'm going to wait until tomorrow night to present this to the Barters so that I can do it in person when they are both at home. Would it be all right with you if I came here after I finish talking with them?

DICK: All right? Of course it will be all right! We'll be chewing our fingernails until you show up!

AGENT: It may be late. I don't know how long it will take at the Barters. Sometimes I have to do an awful lot of talking.

JANE: We'll wait. Even if it means the late, late show.

AGENT: Okay, see you tomorrow night.

*May 24, 9:45 a.m. Tom Sales is on the phone.*

AGENT: Mr. Barter, I wonder if I might come over to see you tonight about the offer I have on your house?

MR. BARTER: Not unless it's 89 thousand.

AGENT: Well, not exactly, but it's *very* interesting. I think you'll be favorably impressed, but I need to go over it with you point by point, and of course we can't possibly do that by phone.

MR. BARTER: You can have twenty minutes. Can you be at my place by 7:30?

AGENT: Certainly, Mr. Barter.

*7:30 p.m. at the Barters'. The agent sits in a single chair facing the coffee table. The Barters are on the couch across from him.*

AGENT: Let me tell you a little bit about these people before we start.

MR. BARTER: Look, what's the offer?

AGENT: No, no. I'm not wasting time, Mr. Barter. It's really important that you know their financial position. You certainly want to be sure that your house won't be tied up and taken off the market for three or four weeks and then have a mortgage fall through.

MRS. BARTER: Oh, dear. I wouldn't want that to happen.

AGENT: Certainly not. And there's no chance of it with these buyers. You see, the husband works for AC&C Computers. He's been there almost ten years and has a secure job. The wife works part-time as a secretary in the local high school. They're looking for a $55,000 mortgage which means their down payment percentage is excellent. It will get them a good interest rate at any of the area banks. Their combined salary is just over $30,000 a year, so they also qualify to carry their mortgage at all the area mortgage lenders. And except for payments on one car and a few charge accounts, they have no large outstanding loans.

MR. BARTER: Sounds like cake and ice cream. How much money are they offering?

AGENT: The offer is $87,000. (*Puts the offer form on the table.*)

MR. BARTER: Look, I said 89 was our lowest figure. Now you want me to come down two thousand more? I think that's asking an awful lot of us. This is a beautiful house. You couldn't possibly build this today for that kind of money. And we've put a lot of hard work of our own into it. And what's all this? *(He picks up the offer form.)* This is ridiculous! They want all this stuff, too? They want to steal this place. You couldn't get all this anywhere in this country for that price. Have you shown these people any other houses at all?

AGENT: As a matter of fact, Mr. Barter, I've shown them many houses. A couple of the ones they looked at have even been sold since they started working with me. Let me show them to you. *(He pulls out five or six listings from his brief-case.)* Here's a colonial two streets up the hill from you. It's got about the same square footage as yours, most of the same features, and the added advantage of a rather level, wholly usable lot. It sold for $85,000 two weeks ago.

MR. BARTER: I know that house. It needs a paint job and it's going to need a new roof. Besides, it has no view.

AGENT: Here's another one in the Fairlawn area. This one sold for $83,500.

MR. BARTER: Yeah? Let me take a look at the listing.

AGENT: Certainly. Would you like to look at a couple of these too, Mrs. Barter?

MRS. BARTER: Well, I guess it wouldn't hurt.

MR. BARTER: You say all of these are *recent* sales?

AGENT: Yes, sir. And I honestly think they indicate that you're getting a very good price for your house. Besides that, my buyers are willing to move the closing up a month. That will save you a whole month's mortgage payment and of course a month's taxes.

MRS. BARTER: That would be good. Then we could go south right away, dear.

MR. BARTER: Listen now. Even if we did consider this offer, we're not going to throw in all this stuff for free.

AGENT: What is it that you object to, Mr. Barter?

MR. BARTER: Well, the freezer for one thing. That's personal property, you know. And we promised it to our daughter. Most of the other stuff we were going to put in the garage sale. They can have the dog pen, nobody would want to move it anyway.

MRS. BARTER: Oh, but they can't have the chandelier. You know how perfect it is for our apartment. I don't think I could ever find another like it. I don't care about the other things, but we really can't sell the chandelier.

MR. BARTER: All right, Martha. We'll keep the chandelier. Look, Mr. ahhhhhh, Sales, tell your people they can have the other stuff, but we have to get $88,000 for our house.

AGENT: Okay, Mr. Barter. Let me just cross out the chandelier and the freezer on this list of extras included and change the price to $88,000. Now all you have to do is sign here and initial the changes. Then I'll go to the Hunters and see if I can't get them to agree to the changes also.

MRS. BARTER: Oh, do you think you'll have any trouble?

AGENT: I don't know, Mrs. Barter, but I'll do my very best for you. Now I want you to understand that this offer form is subject to contracts being drawn by an attorney. This is for everyone's protection. Without that clause, this would be a binding contract. Also I have specified that these contracts must be drawn and signed within one week of this date. This protects you, Mr. Barter, from having your house tied up and off the market because of a contract dispute.

MR. BARTER: Well, you certainly do a thorough job, Mr. Sales.

AGENT: Thank you, I hope I'll be able to complete it by bringing you an initialed copy of this offer form tomorrow morning.

MRS. BARTER: That would be lovely.

MR. BARTER: Yes, we'll be looking forward to seeing you.

*At the home of the Hunters, a half hour later. Dick answers the door.*

DICK: Hello, Tom! We've been waiting for you. How'd it go?

AGENT: Well, I think you've got it.

JANE: At 87? Great!

AGENT: Not exactly. But let's sit down and I'll show you what I have.

JANE: What did they say, Tom? You know 87 is really our very top dollar.

AGENT: They're willing to include all the extras you asked for except the dining room chandelier and the freezer, which they have promised to give to their daughter. So you really make out well. And his counter is at 88.

DICK: This has to stop somewhere. You know we have to set some limits on what we can spend. We're already over our max.

AGENT: Look, Dick, how long a term were you planning to get on your mortgage?

DICK: Most of the banks I spoke with were offering thirty years.

AGENT: Okay. On a thirty-year mortgage an extra thousand dollars costs you $7.69 a month. You really can't let this house go for $7.69 a month, can you?

DICK: Huh, I hadn't thought of it in those terms.

JANE: That's not bad, honey. Tom, do you think the bank will give us the extra thousand?

AGENT: No problem. It hardly changes your down payment percentage.

JANE: Let's do it, Dick. I really love that house.

DICK: Okay. What do we have to sign?

AGENT: Just initial the changes here. You can keep one copy; I'll take one to the Barters tomorrow. Now we have to get the lawyers started on the contracts right away since there's a one-week deadline, and you certainly don't want the house to go back on the market.

JANE: Our lawyer is Al Doolittle.

AGENT: I'll have the Barters' lawyer contact him tomorrow. That'll get things rolling.

DICK: That's fine. And thanks, Tom. You've really done a fine job.

*Handshakes all around.*

Not every negotiation is as complex and sensitive as this

one, but most transactions have at least some of its elements. Sometimes first offers are accepted, sometimes the first counter is accepted, sometimes the haggling goes on even longer. All the participants in this deal were obviously somewhat experienced, and the compromise was reached rather equitably. No one was entirely happy, but no one was pushed too far beyond his limits either. A lawyer friend of mine in Connecticut used to tell me, "If both sides think they've won, or if both sides are crying poor, you've got a good deal." In this case, both buyer and seller were hurting somewhat, yet neither hurt was beyond the limits of satisfaction. Let's look at the "whys" of what happened.

Mr. and Mrs. Barter listed their house on March 3. Mr. Barter felt great pride in a property he had carefully maintained. His asking price was $93,500; he fully expected to get $91,000. Two and a half months passed during which time there was a great deal of traffic through his home, but only one feeble offer of $85,000 from a couple who could just barely qualify for a mortgage at that price. The Barters were feeling somewhat discouraged, tired of the traffic, and anxious to move to the retirement condo which they had already purchased. Mr. Barter was stubbornly determined, however, that he should get a *fair* price for his house.

Dick and Jane Hunter liked the Barters' house the moment they saw it. They were both somewhat tired of house hunting, their house was already sold so they were under some pressure to find a place to live, and the Barter house fulfilled all their needs and most of their wants. The only problem was the price. Between themselves they had set their top-price figure at $85,000 even though they were technically qualified to go somewhat higher in terms of their ability to carry a mortgage. At $85,000, they left themselves money for drapes, carpeting, decorating, and some much-needed new furniture. They made their offer at $83,000 hoping to capitalize on the fact that the house had been for sale for a while, and leaving themselves two thousand dollars to go up to their ideal price.

They were correct in not heeding the agent's initial nudge to duplicate the $85,000 offer that had previously been made on the house. When negotiating, it is often necessary to behave as though you were playing a card game in which it would be self-defeating to indicate a weakness in your hand. In House Hunt, it is defeating to indicate to anyone (especially the agent) a flexibility in price, a willingness to go higher, for you will then surely go there. Let the agent work with the numbers you give him. Do not under any circumstances tell where you are willing to go next. In other words, do not play your next card until after the seller plays his.

Another point: Do not allow an agent to embarrass you into changing your offer. A favorite line is, "I can't possibly present that offer. It would be an insult to the sellers." Occasionally a seller does become insulted by a low offer and refuses to negotiate with that particular buyer, but it is a very rare occasion and usually indicates that the seller is not ready to negotiate with anyone. Also, the agent is required by law to present all legitimate offers. This does not include, "Do you think they'll take _____?" It does include *any* and *every* signed offer accompanied by an earnest-money check.

There are, however, many ways to present an offer. Theoretically it should always be done in person; the agent should go to the home of the seller and present the offer. In practice, this is often not the case. With a rather low first offer, it is not even the ideal. In the case of a low opening, the agent often calls the sellers and makes the offer by phone, a rather impersonal first contact. He fully expects the offer to be refused. He is looking for the reaction of and the amount of flexibility expressed by the seller, and he rarely talks about anything other than the price at this stage. When a first offer is rather close to the asking price, however, the agent will go in person and present all the pertinent information. In the Barter/Hunter case, it would have been detrimental to present financial, mortgage, and closing information at the initial contact stage, since these were strong cards and better played later.

Mr. Barter's refusal to make a counteroffer to the $83,000 offer was also a prudent move. His "Not at that price" was analogous to the pushcart vendor's "You crazy, that's no deal!" It was not a rejection of the buyer, but of the offer. The game at this point is Bid Again. Mr. Barter does not want to start the bargaining at the level proposed by the Hunters. The potential compromise point is too far below his ideal price. He is also looking to see if these are serious buyers or just bargain hunters. His real question is, "Will they bid again?"

Although they had planned on going to $85,000, Dick and Jane are wise to wait overnight before making that their next offer. It is often a good idea to slow negotiation down a bit to allow feelings to cool and rational processes to take over. They come back the next morning with an offer of $85,700. They added the $700 because they were a little uneasy about the outright refusal. They wanted to top the previously refused offer of $85,000, and they thought to themselves that the somewhat unusual figure of $700 would indicate to the sellers that they were not willing to come up too many hundreds more. (Sometimes this works, and sometimes it doesn't.)

Tom Sales then presents this second offer to the Barters by phone. Many, if not most, agents would have chosen a personal visit to the sellers at this point. By the book, that would be the more correct procedure. An agent must judge the emotional atmosphere of each negotiating situation, however, and then adjust his choice of procedure accordingly. In this case, too much contact with the Barters too early in the negotiation would probably have hurt the deal. When he made the second call, Sales was careful to mention the amount of the mortgage, the qualification of the buyers, and the closing date, all factors indicative of a serious and good offer. He was betting that Barter would make a counter. Had Mr. Barter refused again on the phone, Sales would have been in a weak position since he would have had no recourse but to consider the deal "dead." Thus in making the second offer by phone, he was assuming that Barter would not accept the $85,700 figure, and that the

Hunters would be willing to bid again. This may be called "the art of negotiating" or just plain gambling, whichever you choose.

Mr. Barter's counteroffer of $89,000 represents a significant reduction in his price, and he obviously means the figure to be firm. He is forceful almost to the point of belligerence, and his "Not a penny less" sounds very final.

Tom Sales is down to the last few cards. Both parties have indicated that they do not intend to negotiate further on the price. He does not tell Dick Hunter the amount of the counteroffer on the phone but arranges to present it in person where it can be discussed.

Among real estate agents, it is a well-known maxim that you should never take final words as final. Few people mean exactly what they say during negotiation. In fact, a broker whom I know well suggested *Buyers Are Liars* as a title for this book. It was said tongue in cheek and would have had to include *Sellers Are Cheats* as a second line, but there was a grain of necessary truth in the joke.

In this case, the agent takes neither party's word as truth but proceeds to work on an equitable solution to the deal. Now, when the going gets tough, is the time to include the extras. If you must pay more than your ideal figure for the house, then you should try to get more than an empty house. At the same time, moving the closing date up a month is a concession to the sellers, allowing them to close quickly if that is their goal. This can be used in the reverse situation, by delaying the closing date if the sellers need more time. Closing date can often be used by both parties in this way as a part of the negotiation procedure.

The agent is also tactically correct in tearing up the old offer form and redoing it "clean." Now that negotiation is down to its final round, everything should be clear and exact. The offer form to be presented to the sellers should look genuine and firm.

The agent's next problem is to get the opportunity to sit

down with Mr. and Mrs. Barter. Mr. Barter quoted his price as firm and the agent must take care not to put him into a corner where he can only defend his position. He needs the informal atmosphere of the living room and is correct in requesting an appointment with the Barters in their home at this time.

These final negotiating sessions can sometimes be long and complex. Numbers are tossed back and forth and pocket computers are pulled out. Mortgage payment books, scrap paper, financial statements, and comparable listings get strewn across coffee tables. Agents get involved in conversations about the slow rate of sales in the months of July and August, the possibility of the mortgage market tightening up, the cost and inconvenience of moving a lot of the extras in the house, the possibility of the house needing repairs in the next month or so, and the advantages of quick closings, etc., etc.

In the Barter/Hunter case, the agent began by presenting the financial strength of the buyers. When it came to money, he mentioned the figure and then let the neat, newly written offer form speak for him, thus allowing the antagonistic numbers and "extras" to be presented neutrally on paper. In this way he is not the "bearer of bad tidings" and can remain on friendly terms with the sellers. This strengthens his negotiating position.

He follows Mr. Barter's expected negative reaction with the real estate agent's most useful negotiation tool—comparables. Tom Sales shows the sellers listings of houses similar to theirs which have sold in the past year. These listings contain the date of sale and both the asking and the actual selling price. If carefully chosen, they usually make a strong point for a fair price.

Once the sellers soften on price, the negotiations over extras and closing usually work out rather smoothly as trade-offs. The agent also points out the various legal aspects of the offer form before the sellers sign it.

Tom Sales, at this point, is fairly certain that he "has a deal." But buyers and sellers are still a thousand dollars apart on selling price. His approach to the buyers on dollar cost per month per $1,000 mortgage is another standard negotiating tool. When the numbers are as low as $7.69 a month, it rarely fails. So—both parties are hurting a little. It's a good deal.

This is one story. In many ways it's typical and much can be learned from it. But there are almost as many variations on this theme as there were words used in its telling.

One of the most common factors affecting the outcome of an offer is the selling readiness of the sellers. In one particular situation which I remember well, I had an offer which was $5,000 below the asking price. The house was a small, thirty-year-old Cape Cod in need of paint and remodeling and located on a rather busy state road. All things considered, the offer had seemed close enough to me to warrant its presentation in a personal visit. After being greeted at the door by a couple very happy to see me and my offer, we all sat down in the living room. All was warmth and sunshine in the room until I got out the offer form and mentioned the dollar figure. The man sat quietly. The woman burst into a tirade of invective. The offer was an insult, her house was worth much more. I tried very tactfully and quietly to mention the busy highway and the need of paint. Her verbal invective turned to rage. She jumped up and began screaming at me "get out of my house," etc. Fearing bodily harm, I left—quickly! Of course, there was no sale for me. Four months later, however, the house sold for $500 *less* than the initial offer I made.

No amount of expert negotiation could have put together that deal. The sellers were simply not ready to sell at a realistic price. Some deals simply cannot be made. If you come into a situation like this, the best thing to do is spend a few minutes "mourning your losses" and then go out to look for another house.

Time on the market can sometimes be a good indication of how ready a seller is. The agent can often be very helpful here. Some real estate boards print the date of the listing and the date of its expiration clearly on the listing sheet (as in the sample listing of the Barter house given earlier in this chapter, where these dates appear at the bottom of the page). Other boards use codes which convey this information to the agents. Ask the agent when the house came on the market. He is obliged to answer honestly, and he should also tell you if the house had been listed with another real estate office before the current listing. (This usually indicates that there has been some difficulty and/or dissatisfaction.) You can also ask if there have been any offers on the house. The agent is obliged by law to give you whatever information he has. Some listings include a reason for selling. If the owners have already bought another house, you can be pretty sure they're anxious to sell.

Occasionally a seller accepts the first figure which a buyer names. This is often disconcerting to the buyers since they feel "we could have gotten it for less." If this should happen to you, try not to tie yourselves into this emotional knot. Your first offer should have been somewhat below your ideal purchase price, so you have a bargain. The sellers, on the other hand, usually have a figure in mind which you probably hit upon. They therefore are satisfied. Everyone is happy, ergo a good deal.

This very situation happened to me. We had purchased a large parcel of land jointly with another couple. Several months later we decided to list it for sale at a rather high price, almost in jest since we felt it was too early to sell it. I remember riding in our car to dinner with our friends. I turned toward the back seat and said, "Hey, Al, what if somebody offers us $120,000 for the land?" "Why I'd kiss his little toe and sign," said Al. Two months later a sales agent presented a first offer of $120,000. We signed.

Probably the most important factor in an emotionally peaceful negotiation period is your accurate evaluation of the "fair market value" of the house you want to buy. Fortunately there is available an excellent means of determining this figure, although few buyers know of its existence. The tool is the comparables file—the same comparables which Tom Sales used to convince the Barters to sell.

When a house is sold and closed, agents in each office belonging to the board on which it was listed are notified of the actual selling price. They record this figure and the date of closing on the listing sheet. These listing sheets are then filed by town in price order and usually held for two to five years. On some larger boards, they are printed out separately in special comparables books. These comparable sale listings are usually referred to as the comps. Using them is the surest way to avoid overpaying for a house.

"So how do you use them," you ask. When you have found a house that you want to buy, tell your agent you would like to look at the comps. Carefully search the files to find the listings for all the houses of any style in the immediate neighborhood of "your" house, and all the houses of similar style and price in the whole town which have been sold in the past year or so.

Compare the *actual selling price* of the comparables you select from the file with the asking price of "your" house. The points of comparison should include size, age, condition, features, location, lot size, improvements, additions, and extras. After half an hour of search and comparison, you will have an excellent idea of the fair market value of the house in which you are interested. You must then decide upon a realistic "ideal purchase price" and, human nature being what it is, make your first offer somewhat lower.

Those same comps which you selected from the file will probably be used in negotiation with the seller. Whenever there is some difficulty in negotiation, the well-trained agent turns to the comps to make the seller aware of fair market value.

One of the most common ploys used by "super" sales agents to get an offer, or a better offer, is the phrase, "Well, don't wait too long, because I understand there's another party interested in this house." Nine times out of ten, the "other party" is mythical, or perhaps interested but unable to buy. Occasionally, however, he is real. A real other party can often result in a bidding war which can, in turn, result in your paying a higher price for the property.

One of the houses which we ourselves owned had been for sale over a year in a very hard mortgage market. We were despairing of ever selling it at a good price when we suddenly found ourselves with two buyers. The competition bid the price up quite close to our asking price. It is essential in this kind of situation that you decide how high *you* want to go. Ask yourself what the house is worth, *worth to you*. Don't let yourself get carried away with auction spirit.

An agent that I work with had an unusual experience in this type of competitive situation. Two parties made offers at the full asking price that were identical in every way: mortgage, terms, closing, etc. In the three-cornered negotiation, a strong listing agent sided with the real estate firm which had made the first offer. (It was first by a matter of two hours.) This pressure persuaded the seller to accept the first offer because it was first. Checking later with a lawyer, however, the seller discovered that he could have allowed the two interested parties to bid each other up over the actual asking price. Also he was absolutely free to choose whichever offer he wanted for whatever reason he had.

There is one special negotiating situation which you may encounter fairly often in the suburbs surrounding major cities. It is that of the house owned by a holding company. This occurs when a large company transfers an executive who elects to accept a fair market value appraisal price for his house rather than sell it on the open market. The holding company "buys" the house by giving the seller his equity in cash, and then puts the house on the market.

Many buyers feel that these holding companies act much like a construction firm selling a new house; that is, they set the price and hold firm until they get it. This is not an accurate picture. In the first place, the house is almost always listed *above* the fair market value paid to the seller in order to allow room for negotiation. Secondly, the holding company is paid a handling fee by the corporation which has made the transfer, thus providing even more "cushion" in terms of potential profit.

You can and should negotiate with a holding company exactly as you would negotiate with a private seller. The only exception is that the holding company is *always* interested in as quick a closing as possible, so ask for more time than you need when you make your first offer and use the closing date as a negotiation tool.

I could go on at length with stories about the art of negotiating, but perhaps we had better turn now to a closer look at the actual mechanics involved in making the offer. This knowledge is necessary to get you off the ground; it's also necessary to keep you from making a legal error which could cost you thousands of dollars and hundreds of headaches.

In order to make an offer on a house which is under a listing contract, you must give the agent a check. The amount is variable, although $500 is a traditional figure. This sum is termed "earnest money." It indicates essentially that you are a serious buyer who is ready, willing, and able to act. In effect it says, "I want to buy this particular house, and I am not making offers on six different houses at the same time." The agent takes the check with him when he makes the offer and shows it to the seller. He does not *give* it to the seller, however.

The check should always be made out to the broker or firm with whom you are working, not to the sales agent. Write it thus: *Pay to the order of* Joe Welcome, Realtor, trustee. If the offer is accepted, the check is deposited in the broker's trust account and held in escrow until closing. If the offer is refused, your check will be returned to you. If the offer is accepted on the offer form and then one of the parties does not sign the contract, the broker will return your money by check from his trust account. You can lose this money *only* if you sign the contract and *then* decide not to go through with the deal. In that case, the earnest money goes to the seller.

Along with the earnest-money check, you will be asked to sign some kind of offer form. These forms vary from the broker's own printed sheet to the form used to submit the information of deposit to the multiple listing service. The form is called by a variety of names: binder, deposit slip, deposit form, offer form, legal offer form, etc. No matter what it's called or what it looks like, however, it should always contain certain important points. If these items are not included on the form which you are asked to sign, print them in.

1. The names and addresses of the buyer and seller, identified as such, e.g., *Richard and Mary Smith of 10 Pine Court, Terryville, N.J.*

2. The address of the property being sold. If at all possible this should include the lot and block numbers from the town tax maps.

3. The amount of the offer.

4. The amount and kind of mortgage you plan to apply for and the interest rate at which you will accept this mortgage. (Most agents write in "or the prevailing rate," which means that you will accept whatever rate you can get. You are *not* required to add this phrase, however.)

5. The proposed closing and occupancy dates.

6. The extras to be included at the offering price.

7. A statement that a commission of __% is to be paid to the selling broker. (This is really a protection for the broker, but it's best to include it since *you* do not want the transaction dragged through court in a commission battle.)

8. A statement such as: "This offer is valid for a period of *two* days from the above date." This protects you, the buyer, from having the sellers "deliberate" for a week or ten days while you hang in midair.

9. Spaces for legal signatures.

10. MOST IMPORTANT OF ALL: A sentence to the effect of

"This agreement is subject to contracts being drawn by a reputable attorney." *Without this sentence*, the offer form becomes a legal contract when signed by both parties. It is also a good idea to include a cutoff date for those contracts since some attorneys are very slow. Two weeks is more than enough time.

Most real estate agencies have printed contract forms in the office with blanks which can be filled in by the agent. Some salesmen like to "go directly to contract" since the deal is firm when signed by both parties. I urge you *not* to sign one of these contracts without consulting your attorney. I do not mean to imply any trickery on the part of the real estate agents. They are not lawyers, however, no matter how long they have been selling, and the transfer of real property should be handled by a lawyer.

With the offer accepted, the binder signed by both parties, and the earnest-money check deposited, the house is almost yours. The only remaining hurdles are the mortgage, the contract, and the closing. Most banks will require a copy of the contract before making a mortgage commitment; however, they will happily begin application procedures with a copy of the binder in hand. The next step therefore leads us to the banks.

# 7.

# Mortgages

Mortgage money is for sale. It is the stock-in-trade, the wheat, sugar, and coffee of the banking world. As a home buyer, you can, and should, shop for it; for the cost of money, like the cost of any other commodity, is still determined by the age-old law of supply and demand. Because of the competition among financial institutions, you may sometimes find a "bargain," and you can often find a better, less expensive mortgage.

The savings that result from effective mortgage shopping can add up to many hundreds, sometimes even thousands, of dollars, and you'll find that mortgage shopping isn't nearly as exhausting or time-consuming as house hunting. By spending three to five carefully planned hours, you can find the kind of mortgage that is "right" for you and assure yourself of the cheapest money and best terms available in your area.

As we dig into this chapter, you may have the déjà vu experience of thinking, "Didn't I hear this somewhere before?" Well, you did, in chapter 1. Rather than send you flipping back through the pages to those facts and figures, I have repeated some of the basic information which is essential to a more detailed understanding. Most of you will agree that the mortgaging question is complex enough to bear a bit of repetition, and I ask those of you who are "into" numbers to bear with me a while as the rest of us plow through not only getting a mortgage, but getting the *best* mortgage.

Let's get very basic: What is a mortgage? The word comes

from the Old French, *mort gage*, literally, dead pledge. (How about that for seriousness?) Today it has come to mean the conditional transfer or pledging of a piece of property to a creditor as security that a loan will be repaid. A simple statement, but true to the temper of our times, we have managed to add considerable complexity. There are now not only several kinds of mortgages but also special terms, conditions, clauses, stipulations, etc.

To begin with kinds. The simplest kind of mortgage is rarely granted by a lending institution and therefore is virtually unknown to the average home buyer. It is called a straight mortgage. In this situation, a certain amount of money is borrowed for a certain period of time, interest payments are made on specified dates during the term of the mortgage, and at the end of the term, the full original principal is due and payable.

For example, Mr. and Mrs. Tom Jones buy a piece of property from Mr. and Mrs. Henry Fielding for $60,000. The Joneses put down $10,000 and the Fieldings hold a purchase money straight mortgage for $50,000 for ten years at an interest rate of nine percent per year, paid annually. This means that each year on the anniversary of the mortgage, the Joneses will pay the Fieldings $4,500 interest; at the end of ten years, the original $50,000 which they "borrowed" in order to make the purchase will be due and payable.

Although this is not the kind of mortgage you as an average home buyer would ordinarily get or want, I have taken the time to talk about it because of its importance in some special situations. It most often occurs in private financing, that is, financing by an individual. For example, it is commonly used for financing land when the seller agrees to accept a down payment and hold a mortgage on the land for the balance of the purchase price. The term of such a straight mortgage is usually short, perhaps a year, five years, or even ten years, rarely more.

I have also seen straight mortgages used in times of very tight money when the mortgage market at the usual lending institutions was essentially closed. In this case, competent and "creative" real estate agents have been able to "put together the deal" because the seller was willing to hold a short-term straight mortgage for a period of a year or two, or even "until other financing becomes available."

In "normal" times, the kind of mortgage which has enabled the vast majority of homeowners in this country to buy their homes is called an amortizing mortgage. Almost all lending institutions offer it as *the* means of financing a dwelling. To amortize means to apply to a debt for the purpose of settling it. In the case of the amortizing mortgage, the principal is amortized, that is, reduced and finally repaid by applying payments toward it, over a certain period of years.

To illustrate: When an amortizing mortgage is cast, a certain payment is fixed. This figure usually includes principal, interest, and tax payments. It remains the same over the entire period of the mortgage unless adjustments have to be made for increased or decreased taxes. Payments are almost always monthly. Each month some portion of the fixed payment is directly applied to reducing the amount of the loan. The remaining portion pays interest and taxes. In the first years of a mortgage, the payment is primarily interest, with only a small amount going to reduce the principal. As the years go by, however, the principal is gradually diminished because of the monthly payments made toward it. The amount of interest due each month is therefore also reduced. Since the amount of the payment remains fixed, a larger portion of it is applied toward the principal. In such a way, the loan is "paid off" by the end of its term.

All of this is quite complicated mathematically. Fortunately, however, the bank or lending institution which holds your mortgage will send you an annual statement showing how much interest you paid in the course of the year and how much principal remains to be paid on the loan. This information is a necessity when filing your federal income tax return since interest paid on a mortgage is tax deductible.

The amortizing mortgage is so common in this country that if you were to walk into a bank and say to the secretary, "I want an amortizing mortgage," she would probably look at you with a puzzled, uncomprehending expression. She would be unaccustomed to the phrase, for we accept as given that home mortgages are amortizing and call them either just plain mortgages or by their more specific names: conventional, FHA, and VA.

About three-fourths of all home mortgages in the United States are "conventional" mortgages. This means that the lending institution grants the request for a mortgage loan without guarantees or insurance other than the piece of property which is being mortgaged. A down payment of twenty to twenty-five per cent of the purchase price is usually required, although in good times some people with good credit ratings may get a loan with a smaller percentage down.

The conventional mortgage involves the least amount of red tape, and if your credit rating is good and you can carry the monthly payments, it is easiest to get. After you make application for the mortgage, the bank has the property you wish to purchase inspected by their appraiser, checks your employment, checks your credit rating, and if everything is in order, makes a commitment to grant the loan. The process generally takes anywhere from three days to three weeks, depending on how busy and how well staffed the bank is.

Getting an FHA mortgage can take considerably longer (up to eight weeks). More steps and people are involved and each seems to demand a full share of time and "due respect." Speed and efficiency do not seem to be the forte of the federal government.

There is probably more confusion among home buyers about the terms "FHA mortgage" and "FHA approved" than any other single aspect of the House Hunt Game. Despite efforts to inform the public by the FHA, lending institutions, and real estate agents, many buyers still believe that the federal government or the Federal Housing Administration *gives* mortgages and that the approval of a mortgage by the FHA is an endorsement of the quality and condition of a house. Both of these ideas are untrue.

An FHA mortgage is an amortizing mortgage *from a bank or lending institution.* It is like the conventional mortgage in every way except that it is *insured* and *regulated* by the Federal Housing Administration. To get an FHA mortgage, you must approach the same lending institutions as you would for a conventional mortgage. The difference is that you can approach them with as little as five or ten percent down.

The FHA was established by the government during the depression years of the thirties. It was thought then that home building could be encouraged by taking the risk out of mortgage lending. The function of the FHA therefore was to *insure* against the default of the buyer. With an FHA loan there is virtually no risk to the lender. Theoretically this insurance and its alleviation of risk should result in a lower interest rate on the mortgage. The federal government therefore retained the power to set maximum interest rates on the loans which it insured.

Although the maximum allowable interest rate for FHA mortgages is often slightly lower than the generally prevailing rate, these mortgages are almost invariably more expensive to the buyer than conventional financing. In the first place, the buyer pays for the insurance. At this time, the cost of the FHA insurance is ½ of 1 percent of the declining balance of the loan. In other words, if you get an FHA loan at 8½ percent, you also pay an additional ½ of 1 percent for insurance. Your actual payment therefore is identical to the payment on a mortgage at the 9 percent interest rate.

Points also add to the cost of the FHA loan and are another much misunderstood aspect of it. A "point" is one percent of the mortgage amount. If you need a mortgage of $30,000, one point is $300. Points are charged by lending institutions to make the rate of return on a mortgage more appealing. They are paid in advance, at the closing. (This procedure is also sometimes called a discount on the mortgage.)

The FHA allows the lending institution to charge the buyers a maximum of one point. It does not regulate, however, the number of points charged to the seller in order to grant the mortgage. This can run, in times of tight money, to as many as twelve points. In terms of the $30,000 mortgage we just talked about, three, seven, and twelve points would equal $900, $2,100, and $3,600 respectively. Not an inconsiderable amount to ask of the seller.

Despite the fact that these sums are theoretically charged to the seller in an FHA transaction, it is the buyer who actually pays the better part of them. Sellers whose houses fall within the general range of FHA mortgages often inflate their asking price. Early negotiations then focus upon the question, "What kind of a mortgage are they getting?" The price tends to be much more flexible if the answer is "conventional."

Not all elements of an FHA mortgage are costly and negative, however. Low down payment is of course the chief advantage, but also to be considered pluses are the facts that the term can be as long as thirty or thirty-five years and that up to fifteen percent of the loan balance can be repaid per year without prepayment penalty. All FHA mortgages are also assumable. This means that a buyer for your house can save considerable settlement costs and loan origination fees by assuming your mortgage, that is, by paying you in cash the difference between the selling price and the balance due on your mortgage and then taking over your payments. Although few buyers actually have down payments large enough to do this, "assumable mortgage" is a very attractive advertising term in House Hunt.

"But we've seen the term 'FHA approved' advertised. Isn't that another plus to look for in a house?" you ask. No, not if you're looking for a *Good Housekeeping* Guarantee.

Contrary to common usage, the FHA does not "approve" a

house. It *appraises* the property and passes its appraisal information on to the lending institution from which you will get the mortgage, stating the maximum mortgage that it will insure on that property. In the course of the appraisal, the inspecting agent must check many aspects of the house against the FHA's manual of minimal standards. The FHA will not approve the loan unless these standards are met. Often a list of deviations from the standards is sent to the seller, stating that the loan will not be approved unless repairs or changes are made. From this procedure, I believe, came the myth of FHA approval of the property itself.

There is always a maximum on the amount of mortgage which the FHA will insure. This has changed over the years with inflation and is currently set at $60,000 for a single-family dwelling. In some parts of the country where house prices are extremely high, this ceiling can rule out FHA loans for some buyers since they must pay in cash the difference between the mortgage and the price of the house.

The FHA appraisal itself sometimes also rules out an FHA mortgage. This occurs when the appraisal figure is several thousand dollars *less* than the agreed-upon purchase price. The sellers must then agree to lower the price to meet the FHA appraisal figure or the buyer must come up with the additional cash. Here the stress is upon adequate *cash*, since the FHA will not grant a mortgage if the down payment money is borrowed.

Sometimes a seller wishes to speed up the process of an FHA sale by having the house inspected and appraised by the FHA *before* a buyer appears on the scene. This costs him an appraisal fee, but he then has the exact figure at which the FHA will insure a mortgage on his property and needs only to have the future buyer "approved" in terms of credit rating and ability to carry the mortgage. This accelerates the closing process and makes for the common advertising line, "FHA Approved."

Anyone can apply for an FHA mortgage. You should be

aware, however, that it is almost invariably more expensive than conventional financing and that the red tape can be exasperating. Whether you are considering FHA or conventional financing, however, you might want to write for some of the excellent booklets put out by the Department of Housing and Urban Development. Among these are:

| | |
|---|---|
| Home Mortgage Insurance | HUD-43-F |
| Programs for Home Mortgage Insurance | HUD-97-F |
| Wise Home Buying | HUD-267-F |
| Should You Buy or Rent a Home? | HUD-328-F |
| Your Housing Rights | HUD-177-EO |

Send your inquiry to:
Department of Housing & Urban Development
Room B-258
451 Seventh Street, SW
Washington, DC 20410

VA (Veterans Administration) loans have several advantages over FHA loans. Unfortunately, however, not everyone is eligible for them. If either husband or wife served in the armed forces after 1940, you as a couple might be eligible, but the list of dates and qualifications is a long one and you must contact the local office of the VA to inquire about your eligibility. To do this you request Form 26-1880: *Request for Determination of Eligibility and Available Loan Guaranty Entitlement*, and submit it along with a copy of your discharge and separation papers. Do this *before* you start house hunting because the paperwork takes time. If you are eligible, a certificate of eligibility will be issued to you.

Like the FHA, the VA does *not* give loans. Instead, it guarantees them. When a VA-sponsored loan is taken out, the lender is guaranteed $17,500 or sixty percent of the face value of the loan, whichever is less. Since this is not insurance as with the FHA loan, there is no added charge reflected in the interest rate. The VA does set maximum interest rates on its loans, however, and the situation with points is *exactly* the same as with the FHA loan.

With a VA loan, it is possible to buy a house with no down payment. The VA will guarantee a mortgage up to a maximum of $70,000 with no money down if the buyers qualify for the loan. Like the FHA, the VA appraises the property and issues a Certificate of Reasonable Value, which valuation is used rather firmly by lending institutions. It is also required that the buyers submit employment and credit information and the loan application to the VA with a request for the approval of the loan. The VA states that if the "loan conforms to prudent underwriting standards," they will issue a commitment to the lender to guarantee the loan.

All of this procedure takes time, but it is usually well worthwhile, for more liberal terms cannot be found. The VA also has available several excellent booklets on buying and financing houses and operates a *free* home counseling service at most of its regional offices. The address of the local VA office can usually be found in the phone book or write:

Veterans Benefits Office
Veterans Administration
2033 M Street, NW
Washington, DC 20421

As a result of the mortgage crunch of 1974-1975 and the inflation-prompted upward spiral of house prices, there has been considerable pressure among economists, lending institutions, and government financial experts to find new and/or better ways to finance homes. The result has been some government-approved or government-sponsored financial innovations. Among these is the graduated payment mortgage which is being insured by the Department of Housing and Urban Development through the FHA.

The graduated payment mortgage is designed to appeal to the young family with a relatively low "beginners" income and high aspirations. Payments at the outset of the mortgage are considerably lower than on a traditional mortgage. The amount of this payment gradually increases for five or ten years and then remains fixed for the duration of the mortgage term. HUD has approved five different versions of the graduated payment mortgage. Three of these allow payments to increase 2½, 5, or 7½ percent each year for five years and then remain fixed. The other two allow payments to increase 2 or 3 percent annually for the first ten years of the loan.

All five versions of the HUD graduated payment mortgage plan ultimately result in a higher fixed payment than on a traditional mortgage. These plans allow a family to "get started," however, and they rarely cost significantly more in actual out-of-pocket expenditures since the average *real* life of a mortgage in this country is only ten years. (Most mortgages are paid off because the houses are sold. One family out of every five in this country moves each year.)

Another graduated payment mortgage plan is being sponsored by FLIP (Flexible Loan Insurance Program), and low down payment mortgages are also available with private mortgage insurance. Not all lending institutions will grant privately insured mortgage loans, but at those which do participate, mortgages are available with as little as five percent down. There are dollar ceilings on these loans, however, and you must pay a premium for the insurance. The cost of the premium varies from a flat fee, usually about two percent of the mortgage amount, to a continuing payment of about one-half of one percent of the mortgage balance the first year and one-quarter of one percent thereafter.

Another result of the recession of 1974-1975 was the attempt to introduce the variable interest rate mortgage. In this type of mortgaging situation, the interest rate which the borrower must pay each year is determined by the "prevailing rate" among lending institutions. In other words, the interest being charged on the balance of the mortgage will reflect the economic condition of the times rather than remaining fixed. This kind of mortgage is very advantageous to the lending institution since mortgage rates go up *much* more frequently than they go down. It is advantageous to home buyers only when interest rates go down or when a lending institution is more willing to make a larger loan for a longer term because of the flexible rate.

Consumer opposition prompted Congress to pass a resolution against the variable interest rate mortgage at all federal savings and loan associations. These mortgages are available at some state-chartered savings institutions and commercial banks, however.

There is another special mortgage situation, called a balloon mortgage, which is a distant cousin of the graduated payment mortgage and especially appealing to young executives who expect to be transferred by their companies at intervals of two to five years. In this case, a short-term mortgage is written, very commonly, for ten years. The rate of payment, however, is fixed as though the mortgage were being written for a very long term, generally forty or even fifty years. At the end of ten years, the balance of the principal is due in full. This means you must then pay the balance of the amount you borrowed to finance the house. Because of the long term upon which the monthly payment is calculated, most of the principal yet remains to be paid. You can pay it with cash or you can refinance the house. Refinancing is advantageous at this point because inflation will probably have increased the value of the house considerably. The amount you owe then will be a smaller percentage of the value and therefore should get you a better interest rate. There is of course the risk that you may have to sell the house if you cannot get it refinanced. Historically, however, this risk is slight, and I recommend this kind of mortgage for your consideration if you are looking for a little more house than your current income can support with a traditional mortgage.

There is another way to get "more house" which I do not recommend. You may have heard the term "second mortgage"; it is a synonym for "shark waters." Sometimes a buyer needs a larger down payment than he has available and borrows this money with a second mortgage loan. This gives the second mortgage lender a claim on the house after the first mortgage has been satisfied. The interest rates are generally *very* high and the term is usually short, which taken together result in a very high monthly payment. The loan sharks are attracted by the odor of blood, or perhaps by the noise and thrashing of marital discord. Many banks and the FHA will not grant a loan if a second mortgage is used as the down payment, and the VA will do so only under very exceptional circumstances.

If you are having difficulty getting a mortgage or if your real estate sales agent has not been adequately helpful, you may choose to work with a mortgage broker (or banker). This is a specialist whose job is placing mortgages. He charges a fee (usually one percent of the face amount of the mortgage), but he is usually in touch with a wide variety of mortgage money sources and familiar with various mortgage types and options. This is an expensive way to get a mortgage, but the vast majority of mortgage brokers are completely honest and they *do get* the mortgage for you.

One of the favorite questions of buyers who are trying to impress a real estate agent with their "knowledgeability" is, "Does this house have an assumable mortgage?" The question has exactly the reverse effect, and the agent knows instantly that his buyer is new to the game. Very few banks or lending institutions are now writing assumable mortgages, that is, mortgages which can be taken over by the new owner when the house is sold. It is definitely not advantageous to the bank to do so since it is committed to the original interest rate and canot pass on the new buyer's qualifications. Bank executives much prefer, in fact they usually insist on, writing a new loan rather than allowing the assumption.

All FHA and VA mortgages are assumable, however, and if you have a large enough down payment to compensate for the accrued equity of the seller and the inflation-related house appreciation, you may be able to assume the balance of the mortgage at a low interest rate. There are some complex legal questions as to liability on the loan with an assumption, so check this out with an attorney before you enter into this kind of mortgaging situation.

"Open end" is not actually another kind of mortgage since it is simply an option sometimes available with conventional financing. It is important enough and beneficial enough, however, to merit its inclusion here. An open-end mortgage lets you borrow more money on your house, usually up to the original amount of the mortgage, at some point in the future when your payments have decreased the balance due. The interest rate is usually the same as in the original mortgage and there are no refinancing fees. This kind of option may be used to finance major alterations or additions ten or fifteen years down the road, or even a college education. Not all lending institutions will grant an open-end clause, but it's worth the inquiry.

The terms "open" and "closed" mortgage are not related to the term "open-end" mortgage. A closed mortgage is one which cannot be paid off before maturity, that is, before the end of its term. An open mortgage can be paid off at any time.

Most home mortgages are open mortgages. However, many banks and lending institutions write penalty clauses into their mortgages. These clauses provide that a charge will be made if the loan is paid off within a certain short time. The length of time varies from one location to another, but three years is common. The scale of penalty fees is usually three percent of the mortgage balance the first year, two percent in the second year, one percent in the third year, and no prepayment penalty thereafter. Some banks will include a statement in the mortgage that the prepayment penalty will be waived in the event of a company transfer out of the geographical area. Be sure to ask about this waiver if you work for a large nationwide concern.

Now that you are familiar with what you can get in the way of a mortgage, the next logical question is, "Where?" I remember one of our early house hunting experiences during which we were told that "where" was not important. An over-anxious agent tried to sell us a too expensive house using the assurance that he would take us right over to the "mortgage department" of his office and they'd take care of *everything*. Bad news! First of all, this is something of a game, for extremely few, in fact only the *very* largest, real estate offices really have mortgage departments. Helping with financing is the individual responsibility of the individual agent, although the broker or office manager may get into the act if there is some difficulty. Secondly, in letting anyone do *everything* for you, you give up your rights to choose what is being done and to know what is going on. Let the agent help you, by all means; his knowledge of the mortgage market can be invaluable. The final decision as to where you apply for a mortgage, however, should be *yours*.

So where do you begin? When most people think of mortgages, they think of banks. In fact, it is savings and loan associations, particularly those regulated by the Federal Home Loan Bank Board, which are the largest single source of home mortgage money in this country. Savings banks and mutual savings banks are next in importance. If you have an established savings account at a savings bank or a savings and loan association, go there first. Many lending institutions will bend their rules a bit for established depositors.

Commercial banks, or full service banks as they like to call themselves, are not generally a good source of home mortgage money. These banks are more interested in making large loans to developers or for commercial construction. They generally require a larger down payment of the home buyer and their interest rates are generally higher. Sometimes the term which they offer on a mortgage is also shorter.

Life insurance companies often buy mortgages from mortgage brokers as a part of their overall investment policy, but they do not usually deal directly with the general public. Some companies do offer a combined package of mortgage financing and life insurance, which may be beneficial to you if you wish to cover the amount of the mortgage loan with insurance. Check for more information with the company which holds your life insurance policy or with your independent insurance agent.

Surrounding most metropolitan areas you will also find a fair number of mortgage companies. These firms specialize in lending mortgage money. They usually have a rather large variety of "plans" available and are sometimes slightly more lenient on qualification requirements. I have found, however, that there are often hidden costs involved in their mortgages such as large one-time mortgage origination fees or considerably higher-than-average charges for appraisal and credit check. These mortgage companies often send sales representatives on the rounds of area real estate offices, and your agent may have a collection of their cards, calendars, pens, etc. There is, of course, no harm in investigating what they have to offer, but be sure you have a complete list of all charges and do some comparative shopping before you sign the application form.

If you open the Yellow Pages of an urban or suburban phone book to "mortgages," you will find a patchwork list of banks, finance companies, mortgage companies, and individuals. Some of these sources are dead ends since they specialize in second mortgage financing and want nothing to do with the comparatively low interest rate of your first mortgage. Others are indeed potential sources of first mortgage money and deserve a phone call. But there are still other institutions, in fact sometimes the very best sources of home mortgage money, which are not listed under "mortgages." You must therefore flip back to the category "banks" to find their names.

Even if you were to call every phone book entry under both "mortgages" and "banks," you might still miss some of the best money sources. In mortgage shopping, the phone book has the disadvantage of being *local*, whereas lending institutions will often give mortgages in a thirty-, forty-, or even sixty-mile radius of their office. It is the responsibility of the real estate agent, therefore, to have available a list of lending institutions giving good terms in a large geographical area. If he does not have this information, you can spend some time in the local library using its collection of statewide telephone directories as a source of additional names and numbers.

With a list of potential lenders in hand, you are now ready to begin evaluation and comparison. This can get complicated, as any accountant can tell you, for numbers mean different things when added up in different ways, and even then the numbers themselves may not tell the whole story of what is "right" for you. I will try to give you the "facts" about the cost of money. You must add up the dollars and the intangibles, giving more weight to those factors which are most important to you.

Once a buying couple settles on the "right" house, the mortgage, and specifically its interest rate, becomes their chief concern. "What's the best rate we can get?" I hear it every time. They are asking about the price of mortgage money. To most buyers interest rate is the price tag hanging from the mortgage. And yes, it is important, but is is not always an accurate indication of quality. Down payment and qualification requirements, term, and restrictive clauses are the elements which determine the quality.

Almost invariably the interest rate "price tag" is closely related to the down payment. Within any one bank, interest rates will vary depending upon the percentage of the appraised value that you offer as down payment. Let's assume that you wish to use $15,000 as a down payment. This is 50 percent of a $30,000 house, $33^{1}/_{3}$ percent of a $45,000 house, 30 percent of a $50,000 house, etc. In the following chart, you can see how this $15,000 might affect interest rates within the same bank.

| Price of house | % down | Interest rate |
|---|---|---|
| $30,000 | 50 | 8¼% |
| $45,000 | 33⅓ | 8½% |
| $50,000 | 30 | 8¾% |

| Price of house | % down | Interest rate |
|---|---|---|
| $60,000 | 25 | 8¾% |
| $75,000 | 20 | 9% |

If you know the down payment/interest rate relationship in one bank, don't assume that it represents the entire mortgage market in your area. Rates and down payment requirements often vary considerably among banks in the same town. Bank A might give an 8½ percent mortgage with one-third down, whereas Bank B might give the same interest rate with only 30 percent down. Bank A might have a minimum required down payment of 25 percent at its highest rate of 8¾ percent, whereas Bank C might be willing to give a mortgage with only 15 percent down but at a rate of 9 percent.

In the same town, Bank D could have another approach. They might give an 8¾ percent mortgage with only 20 percent down, but the maximum term of their mortgage offering may be twenty-five years, whereas the other banks mentioned might be giving thirty-year mortgages. This difference in term can significantly influence your determination of the quality of the mortgage.

If you plan to remain in your new house permanently, a shorter term may save you several thousand dollars, for you will pay out your mortgage sooner and therefore pay less interest. Your monthly payments will be slightly higher, however. If you plan to sell the house in the near future—three to seven years—you will do well to shop for the longest term possible. Your monthly payments will be lower, and the greater amount of interest paid will be somewhat compensated for by being deductible from your federal income tax.

In mortgage shopping, the cheapest, best, and most beautiful mortgage in the county is of no value to you unless you can "get it." Comparison of qualification requirements therefore is every bit as important as interest rate, down payment, and term.

Exactly how much mortgage money you can borrow depends upon the individual bank, the house you choose, and your personal financial status. Many couples "have heard" that they can buy a house whose price tag is approximately two and a half times their income. This maxim is really rather outdated and provides a "ball park figure" at best. I do not know of a single lending institution using it as a guideline.

I mentioned in chapter 1 that some banks use the guideline of dividing the gross annual family income by either sixty or fifty in order to determine the amount of money available for monthly housing costs. Other lending institutions reverse this process. They multiply the total of principal, interest, and taxes due each month by fifty or sixty. In order to qualify for a mortgage, the gross annual family income must be greater than the result of the multiplication. In other words, if the mortgage you want requires a principal and interest payment of $200 a month and taxes add another $100 a month, your required monthly payment would be $300. Multiply this by fifty and you get a required gross annual income of $15,000.

Some banks use an even simpler guideline. They will grant a mortgage up to 175 percent of the gross annual income of the family. Let's say that together you make $40,000 a year. Such a bank then would grant you a mortgage up to $70,000.

Probably the most commonly used qualification guideline is that one week's combined gross salary minus ten percent must equal one month's mortgage payment including taxes. In this case, if your combined weekly income before deductions is $500, you would subtract $50 (ten percent), leaving $450 as a maximum mortgage payment figure.

These are but a sample of the many methods used for determining qualification. Essentially, each bank has its own, and you may feel that you need a pocket calculator to determine your eligibility at each of the lending institutions which you are considering. Pocket calculators are inexpensive enough, or you may choose the easy way and present the figures to the mortgage officer with whom you are talking and allow him to calculate your eligibility. Do this, however, *before* you make formal application since virtually all applications must be accompanied by sizable application fees.

Remember also that it is the *mortgage,* not the house, that you can or cannot afford. A fortunate couple with $50,000 as a down payment can afford an $80,000 house even if their combined income is only $18,000 a year because they will be carrying a mortgage of only $30,000.

The main concern of the lending institution in qualifying its buyers is to avoid foreclosure proceedings. The bank wants the interest on the money it loans you; they do *not* want your house. If you meet qualification guidelines, the loan officer will look through your application for any large outstanding debts which would require sizable monthly payments. He will also pay close attention to the amount of ready cash which you have. He will ask himself: Where is the down payment money coming from? Is there enough cash on hand in addition to the down payment money to pay closing costs?

Closing costs can add up to hefty dollars. Not long ago it was not uncommon to see a young couple absolutely devastated as they sat at the closing table. The statement of costs and required cash presented to' them by their attorney exceeded by several hundred dollars the sum total remaining in their savings and checking accounts combined. They were about to start life in their new home further in debt than they had expected. It happened all too often, for information about the actual cost of financing and closing was difficult to obtain from banks or lawyers until the very last minute.

Fortunately this tense scene can no longer be played. In the spring of 1974, the federal government enacted a law requiring the advance disclosure to the home buyer of all costs connected with the purchase and financing of a home and the settlement of the title in advance of the closing. The law is called the Real Estate Settlement Procedures Act (RESPA).

In its current version, the law *requires* that the lending institution to which you apply for a mortgage provide a good-faith estimate of the costs of settlement services within three days of the date of the written loan application. It also requires that the lending institution present the home buyer with a copy of HUD's booklet titled, "Settlement Costs: A HUD Guide." This is a carefully researched forty-page booklet covering in detail all facets of closing costs. It includes samples of cost worksheets and the settlement statements which you will see at the closing. You need not wait, however, until you apply for a mortgage to obtain this booklet. I highly recommend that you obtain a copy from:

Superintendent of Documents
Government Printing Office
Washington, DC 20402

It is stock number 023-000-00337-6. The cost is forty-five cents; however, there is a minimum mail order charge of one dollar.

RESPA was enacted to take the mystery out of the real estate settlement process. Settlement fees (or closing costs as they are commonly called in many parts of the country) are really the "hidden costs" of financing a home. Differences in charges and requirements among lending institutions can easily wipe out a one-quarter or one-half percentage point advantage in the interest rate. These fees must therefore be taken into account in order to calculate the cost of the mortgage accurately. You should pay particular attention to one-time charges if you move frequently, since the effect of a lower interest rate is spread over the entire term of the mortgage and therefore will *not* compensate for high initial expenditures on a short-term basis.

A list of settlement-related fees and costs follows. It would be a rare lending institution that would require every item, but I present them all so that you may "Be Prepared!"

1. *Mortgage application fee:* required by virtually all lending institutions. The amount, however, varies widely.

2. *Loan origination fee:* This charge is not regulated and

also varies widely. It is often a percentage of the loan, and it is often higher on small down payment loans. Some institutions do *not* charge a loan origination fee.

3. *Loan discount:* another term for points. This is a one-time charge which increases the yield on a loan and therefore makes the transaction more appealing to the lending institution. Not all mortgages carry points.

4. *Appraisal fee:* another charge which varies significantly from one lender to another. This is the amount which the lender charges in order to cover the cost of an appraisal of the property and a statement of the property value. You have the right to see this report, if you wish.

5. *Credit report fee:* the charge made by the lender to cover the cost of its credit investigation. This fee is not regulated, but usually small.

6. *Lender's inspection fee:* most often applied to new construction when the mortgage application is made on the basis of blueprints. After the house is complete, the lender sends a representative to inspect the property before closing.

7. *Mortgage insurance application fee:* covers the cost of processing the application for private mortgage insurance.

8. *Hazard insurance premium:* most lenders require some form of insurance on the property you are buying in order to protect at least the amount of the mortgage. This may be a straight fire policy or a homeowners policy. Most lending institutions do not *sell* the insurance; however, they require that you bring a copy of the paid policy to the closing.

9. *Survey:* some lenders require that a new survey be done, others will accept the seller's copy of his survey with a statement of no significant change.

10. *Title insurance:* some lenders require that the buyer pay for title insurance for at least the amount of the mortgage. Others do not require title insurance at all.

11. *Pest inspection:* professional inspections for termites or other pests are required by some lending institutions. Re-

quired or not, however, it is probably a good idea to have them done. The fee is small for the peace of mind it buys.

12. *Bank attorney review fee:* some lenders require that their attorney review contracts and closing papers, and the buyer is charged a fee for the review. If you choose to have the bank attorney represent you as buyer also, this fee is usually waived.

If you are still reading this far into this chapter, you'll find actually applying for the mortgage to be a simple chore. When you have selected a lender, obtain two copies of the mortgage application form. (The extra copy will save you a trip to the bank if you should make a major error in completing the form.) These forms are usually credit application–type questionnaires, and you should not have difficulty filling in the blanks. The loan officers are also very willing to "lend a hand" if you have any questions, so don't hesitate to phone them.

When you have completed the loan application, return it to the lending institution with a check for the application fee. You may do this by mail, through the real estate agent, or in person. Most banks prefer the in-person route so that the application can be reviewed by a loan officer while you are there. This allows for clarification of any questions or errors.

Then you leave the bank, take a deep breath, exhale slowly, and try to relax. The loan officer sets the machinery in action. A credit report is requested from whatever credit agency the bank employs. Letters are sent to both husband's and wife's employers requesting confirmation of employment and salary. (If you are self-employed, you will be asked to provide the bank with a copy of the previous year's income tax return.) You or the real estate agent will be asked for a copy of the contract of sale and sometimes for the listing on the house. A bank appraiser will be sent to evaluate the property and present a report of his findings. All of this collected information is then brought before a committee of the bank which passes on the mortgage application.

If your mortgage is approved, you will receive a mortgage commitment from the bank. This is usually a letter which states that the bank will give a mortgage of a certain amount on the property for a given term at a certain rate of interest. The commitment usually carries an expiration date. Ninety days is common; however, if you do not close in that length of time, an extension is usually granted if applied for.

It is usually required that you sign a copy of this commitment letter, signifying your acceptance of the mortgage and terms. Return it to the bank promptly since the commitment letter also carries an expiration date.

You are almost there. At this point, even the most experienced real estate agent heaves a sigh. The deal is firm.

# 8.

# The Contract and the Closing

I've been trying to think of an interesting, entertaining way to present this chapter. I sit at dinner with a far-off stare in my eyes, saying nothing, munching, not knowing what it is I'm munching. My husband looks worried.

"Is something wrong, honey?"

"Oh, ah, no, nothing. How was work today?"

So it goes. Anyway, I've given up. I can't think of anything entertaining about contracts and closings. This would be an easy chapter *not* to write. You've found the house, you've made the deal, you've found the mortgage. What's left is details, procedures, courtesies, safeguards. But if I leave you now, it would be like not saying good-bye after a love affair. Endings are a necessity—on to contracts and the closing.

What's in a real estate contract? Actually it's simply an agreement. Sometimes it starts with a handshake; almost always it becomes a detailed, specific, and somewhat complex written document. Why? There's a great deal of money involved, and people protect their money. Besides money, however, time, convenience and inconvenience, maintenance and condition, personal property, required legal procedures, and often pride and/or stubbornness are also factors in the transfer of real estate. So many strong factors in any situation are an invitation to stress, upheaval, and mortal battle. If you want your "deal" to go smoothly, get a *good* contract.

Many real estate agents have been drawing contracts for years and often are quite competent. A real estate agent, however, is not a lawyer. If you allow him to act as your lawyer and draw your contract for you, and if you later run into contract trouble, he has little or no power to help you. Every buyer thinks and hopes that his deal is an easy one, that *nothing* will go wrong, no problems will surface. It rarely happens that way. I once thought I had an "easy one." Everyone was in agreement, there was plenty of money, no unusual circumstances or demands, and pleasant, reasonable people to work with. What happened? The seller (the husband) had a heart attack *one week* before closing. He lived, but there was intensive care and long nights with a question mark. He and his wife had tremendous pain and tension; the rest of us had severe headaches. So much for my easy deal. I urge you to have an attorney review your contract *before* you sign it.

Also, contrary to what you may hear, there is no such animal as a "standard real estate contract." Everything, *everything* is negotiable. There may be standard procedures that are "customary and usual" in local areas, but they are simply customary and usual and can, at least in theory, be negotiated with the price. Anything on a printed contract form can be struck out, changed, or rewritten, and practically anything can be added.

Although there is no standard contract, there are some standard items which every contract should contain. Be sure yours has the following:

1. The date of the agreement. An absolute necessity.

2. The full name of the sellers, their address, and the designation that they are the sellers and will be referred to as such throughout the contract.

3. The full name of the buyers, their current address, and the designation that they are the buyers and will be referred to as such throughout the contract.

4. The full amount of the purchase price.

5. The type of deed which will convey title. This is the province of the lawyers and I suggest you ask yours to explain about deeds. The "Bargain and Sale Deed, covenant vs.

grantor (or grantor's acts)" is probably the most common. Essentially it means that the seller states that he has done nothing to damage the marketability of the title.

6. The complete address and legal description of the property. The street address and the municipal tax map block and lot numbers are acceptable; a "meets and bounds" description which includes survey points is always preferable, however.

7. A description of how the purchase money is to be paid. This should include the following:

a. The amount of money which accompanied the offer form and is being held in escrow.

b. The amount of additional cash to be deposited upon signing of the contract. The combined binder money and payment upon signing usually total ten percent of the purchase price. This figure is entirely negotiable, however, and can actually be any amount which is agreeable to both parties. Try to make the figure as small as possible. It's your money which is being held without interest.

c. The amount of the mortgage for which you will apply. Also included should be the term of the mortgage, the type of mortgage, and the interest rate which you will accept.

d. The amount of additional cash to be paid by certified check at the closing.

8. A mortgage contingency clause. This is a statement to the effect that the deposit money held in escrow will be refunded and the contract considered void if the buyers cannot get a mortgage as stated in 7c above. The seller's lawyer will be certain to demand that there be a cutoff date for the mortgage contingency. In other words, you will have a limited time to *get* that mortgage commitment. Two or three weeks is customary on a conventional mortgage; try for a month. On FHA or VA, get *at least* six weeks. Don't get into a panic if you are in the process of getting approval on a mortgage and because of bank red tape you overextend the contingency date. It would be a rare occurrence that a contract would be cancelled if you could show that you had proceeded in good faith.

9. The date of closing and the date of possession. Many contracts also contain an agreement on a rental amount in the event of prior possession by the buyer or future retention by the seller.

10. The place where the closing will occur. This may be changed by mutual agreement and very often is, but *someplace* should be designated in the contract.

11. A statement as to who holds the escrow money. Usually either the real estate broker or one of the lawyers is the designated trust agent. In some instances, the escrow money is turned over to the seller after the mortgage is approved and all other contingencies are met. Avoid this if possible, but if the seller insists, it's legal.

12. A provision for termite and/or other inspections and an agreement as to who pays for them. Most contracts contain specific dates by which these inspections must be complete, stating that the buyer waives the right to the inspection if not accomplished by the given date.

13. A statement that to the best of the seller's knowledge the house is structurally sound and the plumbing, heating, and electrical systems are in working order and will be at the time of closing. Some sellers and some attorneys include the opposite of this statement, a clause stating that the seller makes no representation as to the condition of the property and that the buyer is proceeding upon his own inspection. You may have to negotiate over this clause. Try to get a representation of soundness. If the seller's lawyer is adamant against it, make the contract subject to inspection by professionals. In other words, get as much as you can.

14. A list of personal property included in the sale. Be specific about this property. Get right down to curtain rods, shades, light fixtures, rugs. Everything you can think of inside and out that you want or think should stay with the house. One seller, whom I unfortunately worked with, took the mailbox off the post in front of the house, removed every light bulb, *and* despite the fact that the contract stated that living room

draperies *were* included in the price, took the sheer liner drapes which were hung on the inner rod. They avoided detection by having the heavy, patterned outer drapes closed over the windows when my buyers came for the preclosing inspection. No one thought to open the drapes and check underneath. Those sellers moved from Connecticut to Ohio. They received rather unpleasant letters from the buyers, the buyers' lawyer, and me, but they never returned those drapes. They won, finally, by default. It was just too expensive to go into legal proceedings over the draperies. The moral of the story is: List everything that is included in the sale, then check the house carefully the day of the closing; check everything, everywhere, point for point on the contract.

14. A statement that liability for fire or damage by storm or other causes remains upon the seller until closing. Have your lawyer include a statement that in the event of major damage from any source, the buyers may opt for cancellation of the contract with the return of all deposit monies.

15. The amount of the commission and the name of the real estate agency to which it will be paid.

16. The buyers' signatures. It is preferable to have a witness but not absolutely necessary.

17. The seller's signature. Also advisable to have a witness but not absolutely necessary.

Be sure that several copies of the contract are signed. The sheets of paper presented to you as a contract may be photocopies of the typed or printed original; your handwritten signatures upon these sheets, however, make them original contracts. The sellers and buyers should each have a signed original, as should the sellers' attorney and the buyers' attorney. Copies made after contracts are signed will suffice for the real estate agents involved, the lending institution, insurance companies, etc.

Any last-minute changes which are made in the body of the contract, whether they be additions, corrections, or deletions, should always be initialed in the margin by all parties involved. An addendum may also be added to a contract if it is necessary to specify a major change, lengthy clause, or even a list of personal property included in the sale. The addendum is usually a separate sheet attached to the contract. It should be headed by the title, "Addendum to the contract of *date* between *seller* and *buyer*." It *must* be signed or initialed at the bottom by all parties.

While you are thinking about who pays for what closing costs, remember also that lawyers' fees are not regulated. Shop around for the best deal there, too. The real estate agent may be able to recommend a lawyer that he has worked with often, or you may have a friend who has recently closed on a house and felt satisfied with the legal work. Ask at the outset, however, what the fee will be. There's also no harm whatsoever in pulling some lawyers' names at random out of the phone book and asking whoever answers the phone for information as to their standard fee to represent a buyer on a house closing. If nothing more, the calls will give you some standards of cost comparison.

Okay. You have a house, you have a mortgage, you have a lawyer, you have a contract. Sheets get torn off your desk calendar, the closing day arrives. I repeat: *Inspect the house just before closing.* Some buyers go so far as to have the right to inspect the house on the day of the closing written into the contract. It's not a bad idea. When you do go back to reinspect, prepare yourself for a shock. The house which looked so lovely while it was lived in may not be as appealing empty. There is a square of color on the wall for every picture that hung there; there are dirt spots you never noticed on the carpets; and all the rooms look tiny without furniture. Unless you see something contrary to the contractual agreement or structurally amiss, gulp and go on. Elbow grease will remove the dirt spots, and your own furniture will soon make the house your home.

At the closing, you will be paying your attorney for his knowledge and skill. Get your money's worth. Do not hesitate to ask questions about anything and everything. And remember to bring with you the following:

1. Your copy of the contract.

2. Your checkbook with enough money *plus* to cover the expenses projected on the RESPA worksheet.

3. A *certified* check for the cash balance due on the property you are buying. Be sure that this check is made payable to *yourself*. When all the details are worked out, you endorse it over to the sellers or their attorney at the closing table. In this way, you avoid any possible difficulty with the check and the bank in the event that something goes amiss and the property does not close.

4. A copy of your fire or hazard insurance policy if required by the lending institution. Some lenders collect fire insurance premiums with the monthly mortgage payments; in that case they will probably have the policy waiting for you.

In fact, there will be a whole stack of papers waiting for you when you arrive at the closing. Your attorney will have completed a title search and may bring an abstract of the title to the closing with him. The search is done to be certain that there are no defects in the title, and that the seller indeed has the right to sell the property. The abstract is an outline of all the transactions on record which have involved the property.

Some lending institutions require title insurance to protect against faulty title. If required, your attorney will probably have procured it for you before the closing. You will pay for it, however, at the closing. It is a one-time fee and remains in effect as long as you own the house.

If your house is located in a federally designated flood risk area, the lender will also require that you purchase federal flood insurance. This is an annual policy with premiums paid annually.

After most of the papers are signed, you may be required to write a check for interest in advance of the first mortgage payment. This depends upon individual bank policy. You *will* be required to deposit monies on reserve for taxes. A portion of each monthly payment will be added to this reserve account to pay future taxes as they become due. RESPA places limitations on the amount of reserve funds which may be required by the lender, and you can read about reserve fund calculation procedures in the RESPA booklet. Don't hesitate to ask the lender to explain any variance between your own calculation and the figure presented to you. In fact, don't hesitate to question *anything* you don't understand during the closing. I once found a $300 error the bank had made in its figures on a house we were selling. The mistake was in favor of the bank.

As the closing approaches its conclusion, you will grow tired of signing your name. Papers are passed around and around the table to be signed, checks are exchanged. You will hear talk of recording fees, surveys, notary fees, settlement of utility and water charges, tax adjustments, and lawyers' fees. In some cases, you will write individual checks for the fees and adjustments; in others, your lawyer will write the checks, give you an itemized statement of disbursements, and accept your check for the total amount due. No matter how you disburse the money, however, keep enough to allow yourselves to go out for lunch, dinner, or at least a few drinks after it's all over. For *when* it's "all over," you will be just beginning in your new home.

# The Language of the Game

*Absentee ownership*

Refers to real estate which the owner does not occupy or use. This is usually investment property; however, occasionally houses are rented or leased when the owner is to be absent for a specified period of time such as an extended vacation or temporary business transfer.

*Absolute fee simple title*

Title which contains no stipulations, restrictions, or qualifications. This is the best title obtainable, but in reality it is rare in today's world of zoning restrictions and utility easements.

*Abstract of title*

A synopsis of the history of a title, indicating all changes of ownership and including liens, mortgages, charges, encumbrances, encroachments, or any other matter which might affect the title. In some states the buyer is given a copy at the closing.

*Abut*

To touch. Abutting property is adjacent to or bordering another property.

*Acceleration clause*

As applied to mortgages, this clause allows the lender to demand full payment of the loan immediately if any scheduled payment is not made by a given time. It can also give the borrower the right to pay the full amount of the loan before the maturity date without penalty.

## Access

The means of approaching a property. It might be a walkway or a driveway. In the case of a corner property, you might say, "This house has access from _____ Street." In the case of an interior or landlocked piece of property, the access is extremely important and might be a right-of-way or an easement over another property.

## Access right

The right of an owner to enter and leave his property.

## Acre

A measure of land: 43,560 square feet, 38.2 square meters. In square form, an acre of land measures 208.71 feet on each side; however, a piece of property 200 × 200 or 100 × 400 is commonly considered a "builder's acre."

## Affidavit of title

A sworn written statement signed by the seller stating that he owns the property, has clear title to it, and therefore has the right to sell it.

## Agreement of sale

A written agreement by which a buyer agrees to buy and a seller agrees to sell a certain piece of property under the terms and conditions stated therein. Commonly called a contract.

## Amortization

The gradual paying out of a loan through regular fixed payments over a period of time.

## Appraisal

The estimate of a disinterested qualified professional as to the current market value of a property. The term also refers to the report which sets forth the estimate.

### Appreciation

The increase in the value of a property due to inflation or other economic factors.

### As is

A phrase in a contract which implies that the purchaser is buying what he sees with no representation by the seller as to quality or condition.

### Assessed valuation

An evaluation of property by an agency of government for taxation purposes.

### Assessment

A tax or charge on a property to pay for a portion of a specific improvement such as streets, sidewalks, or sewers.

### Bargain and sale deed

A deed which transfers property without any warranties. The most common type of deed.

### Baseboard

The board which skirts the walls of a room at the floor line.

### Baseboard heat

Usually refers to circulating hot water heat through units at the baseboard level.

### Bench mark

A permanent marker in the ground which is used by surveyors to fix property lines.

*Binder*

An agreement to purchase a piece of property involving a small deposit to show good faith. It should *always* include a statement to the effect that the agreement is "subject to formal contracts to be drawn."

*Blanket mortgage*

A mortgage which applies to more than one piece of real estate.

*Bona fide*

In good faith, without deceit or deception.

*Bridging*

Short metal or wood braces for floor joists.

*Building codes*

Rules or laws in a community which regulate the construction of buildings in that community.

*Building lines*

Theoretical lines fixed at a certain distance from the front and sides of a lot beyond which a building cannot project. Sometimes called setback lines.

*Cancellation clause*

Any clause in a contract which allows the buyer or seller to cancel the contract if a certain specified condition or situation occurs. The mortgage contingency is a cancellation clause since it allows the buyer to cancel the contract if he cannot obtain a mortgage.

*Casualty insurance*

Home insurance which covers losses from fire, theft, wind, etc.

## Caveat emptor

A Latin phrase meaning "Let the buyer beware." Legally it means that the buyer is bound to inspect the house and note the conditions which are readily ascertainable. It is the basis for the contract clause which states that the seller makes no representations as to the construction or condition of the house other than what is readily perceived upon inspection.

## Chain of title

A list of all the transfers of title as far back as records are available.

## Chattel

Items of personal property, such as furniture, appliances, chandeliers, which are not permanently affixed to the house. If included in a real estate sale, each piece must be specifically listed in the contract.

## Client

The principal who employs and pays the broker. By definition this is the seller; the buyer is the customer. In practice, however, the buyer is often as much the client as the seller since it is his buying money which pays the commission.

## Closed mortgage

A mortgage which cannot be paid off before maturity. When the mortgagee does accept payment on a closed mortgage before maturity, he usually imposes a penalty fee.

## Closing

The meeting of all concerned parties in order to transfer title. The date when the buyer takes title to the property.

## Closing costs

The expenses over and above the price of the house which must be paid before title is transferred.

### Closing statement
An account of all the expenses, adjustments, and disbursements involved in a real estate transaction.

### Cloud on the title
A defect in the title which may affect the owner's ability to market the property. This might be a lien, a claim, or a judgment.

### Collateral
Security pledged for repayment of a loan.

### Color of Title
A title which appears to be good but in reality has hidden defects.

### Commission
The payment given a real estate broker for his services. Commission is usually paid at the closing. There is no fixed standard of commission, although six percent has become an accepted rate. A different percentage or a given dollar amount can also be agreed upon.

### Concrete
A mixture of cement and sand. If metal rods are inserted in it for strength, it is called reinforced concrete. In basement construction, concrete is usually referred to as a "poured concrete foundation"; on listings it is commonly abbreviated as PC.

### Condominium; condo
Individual ownership of the separate living units in a multi-unit structure with joint ownership of all the areas for public and common use.

### Consideration
Anything of value. A contract must have a consideration in

order to be binding. Because of this requirement, you may sometimes see the phrase "for $1.00 and other consideration" on a deed or contract. The "other consideration" may be many more thousands of dollars in cash or simply love and affection.

### Contract

An agreement between two parties. To be valid a contract must be dated; must be in writing; and must include a consideration, a description of the property, the place and date of delivery of the deed, and all terms and conditions that were mutually agreed upon. It must also be executed (signed) by all concerned parties.

### Conventional mortgage

A mortgage which is not insured or guaranteed by an outside agency or institution.

### Conveyance

The means by which title is transferred. A deed is a conveyance.

### Crawl space

A low-ceiling area usually under a house or part of the house. It substitutes for a full-height (at least seven feet) basement.

### Credit report

A statement of the financial condition of a company. The term is also commonly used to refer to the information which a bank obtains from the creditors of a prospective borrower.

### Cul-de-sac

A street with only one outlet. Popularly called a dead-end street. Most modern cul-de-sacs end in areas where the street is widened to a circle to allow for turning ease.

*Deed*
A written instrument which conveys title to real property.

*Delivery*
The giving of the deed upon the transference of title.

*Depreciation*
The loss in value of real estate, especially because of age, obsolescence, wear and tear, or economic conditions.

*Description of property*
The means of identifying the property which is to be transferred. This may be metes and bounds, government survey, monuments (which includes all identifying boundaries such as streams, walls), tax map block and lot number, street name and number, tract subdivision number, or any combination of these.

*Discount*
The fee charged to grant a mortgage. Also called points.

*Dormers*
Windows cut into the roof and built out to protrude from it. Dormers are characteristic of attic rooms.

*Duplex*
A two-story structure which is divided vertically to house two families side by side, each family occupying both stories.

*Duress*
The use of force or unlawful coercion.

*Earnest money*
A sum of money which accompanies a signed offer to purchase as evidence of good faith. It is almost always a personal

check rather than cash. It can be any amount; however, either $500 or $1000 is customary.

## Easement

A right of way or access. The right of one party to cross or use for some specified purpose the property of another party.

## Eminent domain

The right of a government to take property from a private owner when that property is needed for the "public good." A fair price, which is fixed by professional appraisers, must be paid for the property and the owner must accept this price as just compensation.

## Encroachment

A building or part of a building which extends beyond the boundary of a piece of property and therefore intrudes upon a highway or upon the property of another party.

## Encumbrance

A right or restriction on a property which reduces its value. This might be a claim, lien, liability, or zoning restriction. The report of the title search usually shows all encumbrances.

## Equity

The interest or value which an owner has in a piece of property above the amount of the mortgage and/or other monies owed upon it. For example, the current market value of a property is $50,000. There is a mortgage balance of $30,000 on the property. The owner therefore has $20,000 equity.

## Erosion

The wearing away of land by natural forces, usually water or wind.

*Escrow*

Money or documents held by a third party until specific conditions of an agreement or contract are fulfilled. The earnest money paid by the buyer with the signing of the contract is usually held in escrow until all contingencies in the contract are met.

*Escrow account*

A trust account in which escrow monies are deposited and from which they are disbursed. Both lawyers and real estate brokers maintain escrow accounts.

*Et al.*

Abbreviation of *et alia*, meaning "and others." This term is often used in a contract when a piece of property is owned jointly by several people.

*Et ux.*

Abbreviation for *et uxor*, meaning "and wife." The abbreviation has been widely used in contracts; however, it is preferable and currently more acceptable to write out the names of both the husband and wife in full.

*Exclusive agency*

The appointment of one real estate broker as the sole agent for a piece of property for a specified period of time. In an exclusive agency listing contract the owner reserves the right to sell the property himself without payment of commission.

*Exclusive right to sell*

The granting of the right to sell a property to one real estate broker only. In an exclusive-right-to-sell listing contract, only the assigned broker has the right to sell the property during the period of the contract and the owner must pay the stated commission even if he should sell the property himself during that time.

*Executor*

A person named in a will to carry out its provisions.

*FHA*

Federal Housing Administration, an agency of the federal government that insures lending institutions against loss on certain approved "FHA" loans.

*Fee simple*

*See* Absolute fee simple title

*Fiduciary*

A person acting in a position of trust.

*Firm commitment*

A term used by the FHA when it agrees to insure a mortgage on a specified piece of property with a specified lending institution.

*Fixtures*

Items of personal property that have been permanently attached to the real property and are therefore included in the transfer of real estate. A built-in dishwasher is personal property when purchased new but upon installation becomes a fixture.

*Flashing*

Metal strips placed around roof edges to provide a watertight seal.

*Footing*

The base, usually of poured concrete, upon which the foundation rests.

*Foreclosure*

The selling of a property to satisfy the debt of a mortgage. In order to force the sale, the mortgagee (lender) must file a *Lis Pendens* with the county clerk, thus giving due notice to the mortgagor (borrower).

### Foundation

The supporting walls of a building below the first or ground floor. Cinder block and poured concrete are the most common foundation materials.

### Gable roof

A pitched roof with sloping sides.

### GI loan

A term commonly used to refer to a mortgage guaranteed against loss by the Veterans Administration.

### Grace period

An allowed reasonable length of time to meet a commitment after the specified date of that commitment. For example, most lending institutions allow a two-week grace period after the due date of the mortgage payment before a late fee is imposed.

### Grantee

A person to whom real estate is transferred by deed; the buyer.

### Grantor

A person who conveys title to real estate by deed; the seller.

### Gutters

Half-round or square-shaped pipes made of wood, galvanized iron, steel, or aluminum used to edge pitched roofs in order to collect rainwater and feed it into drainpipes.

### Hand money

*See* Earnest money

*HUD*
Abbreviation for the United States Department of Housing and Urban Development.

*Incumbrance*
Variation in the spelling of *encumbrance.*

*Inspection*
The act of physically observing and testing a piece of property.

*Instrument*
Any written legal document.

*Interest*
A fee paid for the use of money. It is usually calculated as a percentage of the principal.

*Joint tenancy*
Property held by two people with an undivided interest. If one owner dies, the property passes automatically to the other.

*Judgment*
A decree of a court which states that one person is indebted to another and specifies the amount of the debt.

*Landlord*
One who rents or leases his property to another.

*Lease*
A contract which allows one party the possession of real estate for a specified period of time in return for a consideration (usually rent) paid to the other party.

*Lien*
A recorded notice that there is a debt on a piece of property.

This debt could be a judgment, mortgage, back taxes, unpaid accounts, etc.

*Lis Pendens*
Notice of a suit pending.

*Listing*
The employment of a real estate broker to sell a piece of property. A piece of property for sale.

*Littoral*
Having to do with the seashore. Littoral rights are the rights to use the water near the shore.

*Market value*
Generally accepted as the best price that a ready, willing, and able buyer will pay, and the lowest price a ready, willing, and able seller will accept. In other words, the dollar figure at which there is a meeting of the minds.

*Marketable title*
A title which is free from clouds and encumbrances.

*Meeting of the minds*
The mutual agreement of two parties who are ready to enter into a contract.

*Metes and bounds*
*Metes* refers to measures in feet; *bounds* refers to direction in degrees. Together they are used to give a legal description of the boundaries of a piece of property after that property has been surveyed.

*Mill*
Equal to one-tenth of one cent. A mill is the unit of measure for property taxation rates.

*Model home*

A completed house which a developer promises to duplicate at a given price on another lot of the tract.

*Mortgage*

A legal document which creates a lien upon a piece of property.

*Mortgage commitment*

A written statement from a lender to grant a mortgage upon a specified piece of property under specified terms. Mortgage commitments are usually made for a certain period of days although they can often be renewed if the transaction has not closed within the time of the original term. Ninety days is an average length of time.

*Mortgagee*

The party or institution which lends the money.

*Mortgagor*

The persons or party which borrows the money, giving a lien on the property as security for the loan.

*Multiple listing*

An arrangement among real estate brokers to make their listings available to each other. If a sale results, the agreed-upon commission is divided between the listing broker and the selling broker.

*Notary public*

A person licensed to authenticate documents and certain transactions.

*Offer*

A proposal, oral or written, to buy a piece of property at a specified price.

*Open-end mortgage*

A mortgage which can be paid off before the maturity date without penalty and which can be refinanced up to the original amount.

*Overhang*

Part of the roof which extends beyond the walls of a building.

*Parquet floor*

Hardwood floors laid in small squares or other repeating patterns.

*Percolation test; perc test*

An evaluation of the drainage capability of the land. A perc test is an absolute necessity when buying land which will require a septic system, and the contract should be contingent upon the satisfactory report of the test.

*Personal property*

Also termed *personalty*. Anything that is not permanently attached to the real property. Chandeliers, mirrors, and drapery rods are common examples.

*Points*

Sometimes called *discount*. This is a fee which the lending institution charges for the mortgage. One point is one percent of the face amount of the mortgage.

*Power of attorney*

An instrument in writing that gives one person the right to act as an agent for another in signing papers, deeds, documents, etc.

*Purchase money mortgage*

A mortgage which is "taken back" by the seller in an amount

which is the difference between the down payment and the agreed-upon purchase price. For example, a piece of property sells for $80,000. The buyers have a down payment of $30,000. The sellers take back a purchase money mortgage on the property for $50,000. This arrangement occurs most often in the sale of undeveloped land or hard-to-sell properties.

### Qualifying a buyer

The real estate agent's process of checking out the buying potential of a customer. It is necessary to know family income, available down payment money, and all outstanding debts in order to accurately "qualify" a buyer.

### Real property

Land and buildings and anything permanently attached to the land and/or buildings.

### Realtor

A real estate broker who is a member of the National Association of Realtors.

### Regular lot

A rectangular lot.

### Report of title

A document required before title insurance can be issued. It states the name of the owner, a legal description of the property, and the status of taxes, liens, and anything else which might affect the marketability of the title.

### Restriction

A limitation to control the use of a piece of property.

### Right of way

An easement; the right of one party to cross or in some way use the property of another party.

*Riparian rights*

The right to use the water (rivers, lakes, streams) that borders an owner's land.

*Septic tank*

A private sewage disposal system for an individual home. A large concrete tank is buried underground. Waste water flows into the tank, where solid matter settles and decomposes, leaving the water to flow out of the tank into a system of gravel beds. Land with good drainage is essential to the efficient operation of a septic system.

*Setback*

A specific distance set by municipal ordinance which must remain between a building and the boundaries of a lot. Most often used to refer to the distance between the curb and the front of a building.

*Sheetrock*

Sheets of composite materials used for interior walls and ceilings instead of wet plaster on wire mesh. Called drywall construction and used in practically all modern construction.

*Siding*

The finished cover on the outside walls of a building. Common materials are cedar shingles, wood clapboard, Masonite-type clapboard, aluminum, vinyl, and brick.

*Specific performance*

A court order which compels a party to carry out the terms of an executed (signed) contract.

*Subdivision*

A tract of land broken into smaller lots usually for the purpose of building houses. Often used as a synonym for a "development."

*Sump pump*

An automatic water pump set in the basement floor to prevent groundwater from seeping into the basement.

*Survey*

The measurement of a piece of land by civil engineers or surveyors to determine its area and attest to its boundaries.

*Tenant*

A person or party who rents or leases property from a landlord.

*"Time is of the essence"*

A phrase used in a contract to indicate that specific dates are essential to the contract and that the contract terms must be performed on those dates. It is most often used in regard to closing dates.

*Title*

Actual ownership; the right of possession; evidence of ownership.

*Title insurance*

An insurance policy which protects against loss incurred because of defective title. A title search is always required before the title insurance is granted.

*Title search*

A professional examination of public records to determine the chain of ownership of a particular piece of property and to note any liens, mortgages, encumbrances, easements, restrictions, or other factors which might affect the title.

*Usury*

Charging a higher rate of interest than is legally allowed.

### VA

Abbreviation for Veterans Administration, an office of the United States government which can guarantee home mortgage loans for certain veteran-approved lending institutions.

### Valuation

Estimated or determined value.

### Variance

An exception to a zoning ordinance granted to meet certain specific needs.

### Void

Cancelled; not legally enforceable.

### Waiver

The renunciation or surrender of a right, privilege, or specified agreement.

### Warranty deed

The best deed because it contains the agreement that the seller (grantor) will protect the buyer (grantee) against any claimant. In common practice, however, this deed is not often given.

### Water table

The natural level of water below the surface of the ground. A high water table can mean damp basements and/or septic system problems.

### Zoning ordinances

Municipal ordinances which limit and regulate the character and uses of private property in a given area.